# They Are Ok

*by*
*John Hughes*

***Published by: Writer Cosmos***

ISBN (PB): 979-8-89604-284-6

ISBN (HB): 979-8-89604-285-3

# Disclaimer

*This book is a work of narrative non-fiction. While it is based on real events and people, certain names and identifying details have been changed to protect the privacy of individuals. In crafting these stories, the author has ensured factual integrity and respectful representation.*

*The author has made every effort to accurately portray events, conversations, and experiences as they happened. However, some dialogue or scenes may have been reconstructed or adapted for clarity, flow, or literary effect.*

# Table of Contents

# Dedication

*To all those I've had the privilege to meet when they needed to know 'Are They OK'.*

*The seekers, the broken-hearted, the brave souls who sat across from me with open hearts, searching for peace in the midst of grief, this book is dedicated to you.*

*Thank you for trusting me with your stories, your tears, and your hopes.*

*It has been my deepest honour to walk with you, if only for a while, on your journey towards healing.*

*'They Are OK.'*

# Acknowledgements

My heartfelt thanks to the researchers whose insight and dedication helped bring clarity and depth to these pages, and to the publishing team whose care and expertise guided this book into the world. Your contributions have been invaluable.

To my friends, family, and spiritual mentors who encouraged me, listened patiently, and reminded me why this work matters, your love and insight carried me through the challenging moments.

And to my spirit guide, for the quiet guidance and presence that was felt in every word, every pause, every message received, I am forever humbled to serve.

# About the Author

John Hughes is an internationally recognised award-winning Psychic Medium whose extraordinary gift has brought comfort, hope, and healing to thousands across the globe. With a career spanning decades, John has become a trusted voice in the world of spiritual communication, renowned for his compassionate approach and uncanny ability to connect with those who have passed. His work has been featured on many television programmes, where his profound insights and heartfelt messages have touched audiences from all walks of life.

John's passion for helping others through grief stems from his own personal journey and the countless stories he has witnessed in his work. His commitment to serving the bereaved is rooted in a deep belief: that love never dies, and that our connection to those we've lost continues beyond the veil.

In *They Are OK*, John offers a tender and transformative guide for anyone navigating loss, blending practical advice with spiritual wisdom. With every page, his warmth, empathy, and intuitive understanding shine through. He makes the invisible world of spirit feel present and real.

John continues to work as a medium, teacher, and speaker, offering one-on-one readings, workshops, and public demonstrations. His mission remains clear: to remind the living that their loved ones are ever present, watching over them.

# Author's Note

As a psychic medium, I, John Hughes, have dedicated my life to bridging the gap between the physical and spiritual realms.

My journey into the world of spiritual communication began many years ago, driven by a profound desire to understand and connect with the unseen energies that surround us. Along the way, I have cultivated a deep sense of empathy and a powerful ability to connect with those who have crossed over, offering comfort and guidance to the living.

Coping with the death of a loved one is an experience for which no one is ever truly prepared. The pain and sense of loss can be overwhelming, often leaving one feeling isolated and adrift. In these moments of profound grief, my role as a psychic medium becomes especially important. It is my calling to help you navigate the turbulent waters of sorrow and to find solace in the messages and presence of your departed loved ones.

Those who come to see me often say they have found a safe and compassionate space—one where their grief is acknowledged, honoured, and respected. Through my mediumship, I facilitate communication between you and those who have passed on, offering evidence of their continued existence and their enduring love for you. These connections can be profoundly healing. They help in bringing closure to unresolved matters and reaffirming the unbreakable bonds that death cannot sever.

One of the most moving aspects of my work is witnessing the transformation that occurs when someone connects with a loved one on the other side. The messages I convey frequently include specific details and cherished memories that only you and your loved one would know, validating their presence and bringing a deep sense of peace. These moments allow the focus to shift—from loss to the lasting relationship you still share.

Grief is a journey, and while the pain may never fully disappear, understanding that your loved ones remain with you in spirit can ease the burden considerably. They continue to watch over you, guide and support you from beyond the physical world. My purpose is to serve as a conduit for their messages, helping you feel their presence and love in your everyday life.

As a psychic medium, my mission is not only to connect you with those who have passed, but also to assist you in finding a path toward healing and acceptance. Death is not an end, but a transition—and by embracing this truth, we can move forward with renewed purpose and a deeper appreciation for the interconnectedness of all life.

If you are struggling with the loss of a loved one, please know that you are not alone. I am here to support you, offer insight and connection to guide you through the darkness of grief. Together, we can find peace, comfort, and a reaffirmation of the eternal bonds of love that transcend even death.

# Introduction

Losing a loved one is a profound and life-altering experience. The journey through grief can be overwhelming, confusing, and isolating. This book is intended as a companion on that journey, offering guidance, comfort, and practical advice for navigating the complex emotions and challenges that come with loss.

The death of a loved one can leave an indelible mark on our hearts, plunging us into a deep sea of sorrow and longing. Amid this emotional turmoil, many seek solace and understanding through various means, including spiritual guidance. One avenue that some find particularly comforting is consulting with a psychic. Psychics, believed to possess heightened intuitive abilities, can offer unique insights and support during the grieving process.

One of the most profound ways a psychic may help is by fostering a sense of connection with the departed. Psychics relay messages from the other side. For those who are grieving, receiving a message from a lost loved one can bring immense comfort. It can reaffirm the belief that their spirit continues to exist, offering reassurance that they remain present in some form. This connection can ease the pain of separation and nurture a continued sense of relationship with the deceased.

Unresolved questions and emotions often accompany the death of a loved one. A psychic reading may offer closure by addressing these lingering concerns. Whether it's understanding the circumstances of their passing, expressing unspoken sentiments, or receiving affirmations of love and forgiveness, a psychic can facilitate a dialogue that brings peace. This sense of closure can be instrumental in the healing process, helping to resolve emotional and psychological conflicts that may otherwise hinder recovery.

Grief can be a lonely path, and feelings of isolation are common. A psychic can provide validation and affirmation of your experiences and emotions. By tuning into your energy and that of your loved one, they can offer insights that resonate deeply, confirming your feelings and experiences. This validation can be profoundly healing, acknowledging the reality and significance of your grief and affirming that your loved one is at peace.

For many, the loss of a loved one prompts deep existential questions about life, death, and afterlife. A psychic may help deepen your spiritual understanding by sharing insights into these profound mysteries. Their experiences of the spiritual realm can support you in exploring your beliefs and expanding your consciousness. This deeper awareness can provide comfort and perspective, making the experience of loss more bearable and less frightening.

Grieving is a deeply personal process that varies from person to person. While consulting a psychic may not appeal to everyone, for those who are open to it, it can be a powerful source of comfort and healing. By offering connection, closure, emotional validation, spiritual guidance, and hope, a psychic may play a valuable role in supporting you through your journey of loss. Embracing this form of spiritual support can help foster inner peace and acceptance, allowing you to honour your loved one's memory while finding your own path to healing.

## Chapter 1: Understanding Grief

This chapter explores the nature of grief. We will discuss the various stages of grief as conceptualised by experts such as Elisabeth Kübler-Ross and examine how grief manifests differently in everyone. Understanding these stages and recognising that grief is a personal and non-linear process can help lay the foundation for healing.

## Chapter 2: The Immediate Aftermath

The days and weeks following a loss can be chaotic and disorienting. We will cover the practical and emotional challenges that arise immediately after a loved one's death, including making funeral arrangements, responding to condolences, and coping with the initial shock and disbelief.

## Chapter 3: The Emotional Rollercoaster

Grief is an emotional rollercoaster, with unpredictable and often intense highs and lows. This chapter delves into the wide range of emotions one might experience, such as sadness, anger, guilt, and even relief. We will offer strategies for managing these feelings and emphasise the importance of allowing yourself to grieve fully.

## Chapter 4: Physical and Mental Health

Grief affects not only your emotions but also your physical and mental well-being. We will discuss common physical symptoms—such as fatigue and appetite changes—as well as mental health challenges like anxiety and depression. Tips for self-care and recognising when to seek expert help will be included.

## Chapter 5: The Role of Support Systems

No one should grieve alone. This chapter underscores the importance of leaning on family, friends, and support groups. We will explore how to express your needs and accept help when offered, as well as the benefits of joining a grief support group and connecting with others who truly understand.

## Chapter 6: Honouring and Remembering

Finding ways to honour and remember your loved one is a crucial part of the healing process. We will share ideas for preserving their memory, including creating memorials, commemorating anniversaries, and establishing personal rituals that bring comfort.

## Chapter 7: Navigating Special Days

Holidays, birthdays, and anniversaries can be especially difficult following a loss. This chapter offers practical advice for coping with these emotionally charged times, including preparation strategies and suggestions for creating new traditions that both honour your loved one and bring moments of joy.

## Chapter 8: Moving Forward

Moving forward does not mean forgetting. It means learning to live with the loss and establishing a new sense of normal. We will explore the concept of "continuing bonds," maintaining a connection with your loved one while slowly rebuilding your life, and how to find renewed meaning and purpose.

## Chapter 9: Seeking Professional Help

Sometimes, grief becomes too heavy to bear alone. This chapter provides guidance on seeking support from a specialist, including different therapy options, how to find a grief counsellor, and what to expect from the therapeutic process. We'll discuss the signs that indicate it's time to seek help and the potential benefits of doing so.

## Chapter 10: Stories of Hope and Healing

Grief is universal, yet every journey is unique. In this chapter, we share stories of individuals who have travelled through the darkest depths of grief and found hope and healing. These narratives are a testament to the resilience of the human spirit and the possibility of finding light after loss.

## Chapter 11: The Unthinkable Loss – Losing a Child and Learning to Breathe Again

There are no words strong enough—no metaphors gentle enough—to fully capture what it means to lose a child. It is a heartbreak that shatters time. The world continues to turn, but something vital inside you stops. The air feels thinner. Colours seem duller. Even your own reflection appears unfamiliar. You are still here—but you are no longer the same. You never will be.

## Chapter 12: Grief, Spirit Messages, and the Sensitivity of Children

This chapter explores the often-overlooked connection between grief, spiritual sensitivity, and the innate openness of children. While adults may intellectualise loss or second-guess signs from the beyond, children often experience grief—and spirit connection—intuitively. They might mention dreams, imaginary conversations, or sudden waves of comfort that appear from nowhere. Rather than dismiss these experiences, this chapter invites readers to honour and embrace them.

## Chapter 13: There Is No Required Waiting Period for Love

Grief has no rules. That is one of the first things I learned. Some people expect you to grieve according to a timeline, moving through the "stages" as though progressing through levels of a video game. Others don't know what to say, so they say nothing at all. This chapter reminds us that grief is deeply personal and that love, healing, and joy can re-emerge in their own time—and that's perfectly okay.

# Chapter One

## *Understanding Grief - The Silence of His Voice*

The first thing I noticed was the silence. My father's voice—once a constant presence in my life—was gone. The house felt empty, even though it was filled with the usual sounds of daily life. His favourite chair, the one he always occupied during family gatherings, now seemed like a gaping void in the living room. Grief is an unwelcome guest. It arrives uninvited, settles into your life, and alters everything in its wake.

My father passed away on a cold, wet night in May. The sky wept with us, and as the news spread among family and friends, so did the tears. He had been the voice of reason in times of chaos, a comforting presence in all our lives. He was always the one to offer advice—the person we turned to in troubled times. He had been the cornerstone of our family, holding us together with his wisdom and strength. Losing him felt like losing the very foundation upon which our lives were built. It was as though a part of ourselves had been torn away, and we were left to navigate the turbulent waters of grief alone.

Grief is not a linear process. It doesn't follow a predictable path or timeline. It strikes in waves—sometimes gentle, sometimes overwhelming. The days following his death were a blur of funeral arrangements, condolences, and a deep, pervasive sadness. I remember standing in the funeral home, the scent of flowers heavy in the air, feeling utterly lost and alone. How do you say goodbye to someone who was such an integral part of your life?

Amidst the sorrow, there were moments of laughter too. We shared stories about my father, reminiscing about his quirks, his kindness, and his fierce love. These memories were like little lifeboats, keeping us afloat during the storm. But as days turned into weeks, and weeks into months, the reality of his absence began to sink in. The initial flurry of support faded, and we were left to face our grief in the quiet of our own lives.

Grief affects everyone differently. For some, it manifests as deep, unrelenting sadness. For others, it may take the form of anger, confusion, or guilt. I experienced all of these emotions—and more. There were days when getting out of bed felt impossible. On several nights, sleep became a distant memory. The world had changed, and I was struggling to find my place in it without him.

One of the most difficult aspects of grieving is the sense of isolation. People mean well, but unless they've experienced such loss themselves, they can't truly understand what you're going through. Phrases like "he's in a better place" or "time heals all wounds" felt hollow and unhelpful. What I really needed was someone to listen, someone who would let me cry and simply sit with me in my pain.

After my father's death, I found myself adrift in a sea of grief, desperately searching for something to anchor me. The silence in our home was deafening, and my heart ached with the absence of his comforting presence. It was during this time of profound loss and confusion that I began to turn inward, seeking solace in spirituality—a path I had never seriously considered before.

Growing up, spirituality had always seemed abstract—something other people engaged in, but not something that played a tangible role in my life. My father had been a practical man, grounded in the here and now, and our family was never particularly religious. Yet, in the wake of his passing, I felt an inexplicable pull towards exploring the spiritual realm, as though something beyond my understanding was calling out to me.

One evening, feeling especially lost, I wandered into a small bookshop I had passed countless times but never entered. Drawn to a corner filled with books on spirituality, meditation, and the afterlife, I picked up a book on communicating with the spirit world. Sceptical but hopeful, I decided to give it a try. I needed to believe that my father's spirit was still with me in some way—that our bond transcended the physical world.

I began to meditate in my own way, focusing on quieting my mind and opening myself to whatever messages might come through. At first, it felt awkward and forced, but gradually, a sense of peace began to settle over me during those moments. I found comfort in the thought that my father could still hear me—that he was watching over me from somewhere beyond.

One night, while deep in thought, I felt a sudden warmth envelop me—a sensation so profound and comforting that it brought tears to my eyes. In that moment, I sensed my father's presence more strongly than ever before. It was as though he were sitting beside me, reassuring me with his familiar, steady presence. I could almost hear his voice, encouraging me to keep moving forward, to live my life fully and without fear.

These experiences deepened my belief in the spirit world and convinced me that our loved ones never truly leave us. They remain connected to us in ways that may not always be visible but are deeply real. I began to seek out others who had experienced something similar, eventually joining a local spiritual group where people shared their own connections with the other side. Their stories resonated with me, affirming that I was not alone in this journey.

As I continued to explore spirituality, I learned to trust my intuition and the subtle signs that seemed to come from my father—a familiar song on the radio, a sudden breeze on a still day, or the feeling of his hand on my shoulder when I needed it most. These were his ways of communicating with me, reminding me that he was still part of my life.

Attending that first spiritual meeting marked a turning point. It opened my heart to the possibility of communicating with the spirit world and offered the peace and understanding I had been yearning for. Through this journey, I discovered that our loved ones remain with us—not in body, but in spirit, in memory, and in love.

Turning to spirituality after my father's death brought me a sense of peace and clarity I had never known. It helped me to accept his passing, knowing our connection was eternal. I came to see that the spirit world is not a distant or unreachable place, but one that exists alongside our own—filled with love and the enduring presence of those we hold dear.

Loss is a road that winds endlessly without a map to guide you. There are good days and bad days, moments of joy and sorrow. But through it all, I've learnt that it's okay to ask for help. It's okay to lean on others and to allow yourself to feel whatever it is you're feeling. Grief is a testament to the love we carry for those we've lost. While it never truly disappears, it transforms and evolves over time.

The empty chair in our living room is still a painful reminder of my father's absence, but it's also a symbol of the love and memories we shared. As I continue to navigate this new reality, I hold on to the knowledge that he will always be a part of me—and that it's okay to grieve, to remember, and to find joy again.

Grief is a complex and multifaceted emotional response to loss. It can be overwhelming, disorienting, and deeply personal. Understanding grief is the first step in navigating this difficult journey. In this chapter, we will explore the nature of grief, its stages and types, and the many ways it can manifest.

Grief is the natural reaction to losing someone or something significant. It encompasses a wide range of emotions—from deep sorrow to anger and disbelief. The intensity and duration of grief vary greatly from person to person, influenced by factors such as the nature of the loss, the closeness of the relationship, and individual coping mechanisms.

There are recognised stages of grief that many people experience. These stages may come in waves and may not follow a specific order, but they are common when we lose someone or something deeply cherished.

**Denial** is usually the initial stage. It helps to numb the shock of loss and acts as a temporary buffer against overwhelming emotions.

**Anger** follows as the denial fades and pain surfaces. This anger may be directed at oneself, others, or even at the deceased for leaving.

**Bargaining** comes next, often filled with "what ifs" and "if only" thoughts—an attempt to regain a sense of control and to make sense of the loss.

Sometimes, the anger that accompanies loss—interwoven with the many other emotions of grief—can prevent a person from moving forward or seeing clearly enough to process their emotions objectively. Taking even a brief moment to clear your mind, to invite stillness, and to create space for peace and positivity can help cultivate a more hopeful outlook for the future.

**Depression** may descend as the second last stage, and a profound sadness can take hold as the reality of the loss becomes undeniable. This stage is often marked by feelings of desolation and despair.

Then comes the final stage, **acceptance**—not a return to happiness, but a beginning of learning to live with the loss and move forward.

Grief is a testament to the love and connection we shared with the person who has passed away. While it is one of life's most difficult experiences, understanding its nature can help us navigate the journey with greater awareness and resilience. In the following chapters, we will explore the practical aspects of coping with grief—from the immediate aftermath of a loss to discovering ways to rebuild our lives. It's also important to understand that grief can take many forms, some of which are often misunderstood or overlooked:

## Types of Grief:

- **Anticipatory Grief**: *This arises when a loss is expected, such as during a terminal illness. It involves mourning before the actual loss occurs.*
- **Normal Grief**: *The typical response to loss, encompassing a range of emotional, physical, and cognitive reactions that gradually subside with time.*
- **Complicated Grief**: *Also known as prolonged grief disorder, this involves intense and persistent mourning that severely impairs daily functioning.*
- **Disenfranchised Grief**: *Grief that is not acknowledged or validated by society, such as the loss of a former partner, a pet, or through miscarriage.*
- **Secondary Losses**: *These are additional losses triggered by the primary loss, such as the loss of a role, identity, or future plans.*

Grief impacts every aspect of a person's being—emotionally, physically, mentally, and spiritually. Common manifestations include:

- **Emotional**: *Intense sadness, anger, guilt, anxiety, loneliness, and even relief.*
- **Physical**: *Fatigue, appetite changes, sleep disturbances, physical aches, and a weakened immune system.*
- **Mental**: *Difficulty concentrating, memory lapses, confusion, and obsessive thoughts about the loss.*
- **Spiritual**: *Questioning one's beliefs, struggling to find meaning, or feeling disconnected from previously held faith or values.*

## Strategies for Managing Grief:

- **Allow Yourself to Grieve**: *Give yourself permission to feel and express your emotions. Crying or feeling low is not a sign of weakness—it's part of healing.*
- **Seek Support**: *Reach out to friends, family, or support groups who can provide empathy and understanding.*
- **Prioritise Self-Care**: *Maintain your physical health through proper nutrition, exercise, and rest.*
- **Find Healthy Outlets**: *Express your emotions through journalling, art, talking to a therapist, or engaging in meaningful activities.*
- **Honour Your Loved One**: *Create rituals or find personal ways to commemorate and celebrate the life of the person you've lost.*

Grief is a deeply individual journey. There is no set timeline, and healing does not follow a straight path. Practising patience and self-compassion is essential. Understand that setbacks are normal, and progress often comes gradually.

During periods of grief, self-criticism and guilt can easily take hold. You may question whether you're grieving "properly" or become frustrated with your perceived lack of progress. Practising self-compassion means treating yourself with the same kindness and care you would extend to a friend facing similar pain.

## Embracing Self-Compassion:

- **Recognising Your Humanity**: *Grieving is a fundamental part of being human. Feelings of pain, confusion, or numbness are natural and do not signify weakness—they reflect the depth of your love and the significance of your loss.*
- **Allowing Yourself to Feel**: *Society often encourages us to "stay strong" or "move on". Self-compassion invites you to fully experience your emotions without rushing to suppress them. It's okay to cry, to be angry, or to feel broken. These are all part of the healing process.*
- **Forgiving Yourself**: *You may find yourself replaying moments or wishing you had acted differently. Practise forgiveness, and remember that*

*hindsight brings clarity we didn't have in the moment. You did the best you could with what you knew then.*

- **Attending to Your Needs**: *Self-compassion includes caring for your physical and emotional well-being. This might involve rest, nutritious meals, experienced support, or engaging in comforting activities. Looking after yourself is not indulgent—it's a necessary part of recovery.*

## Integrating Patience and Self-Compassion:

- **Mindful Reflection**: *Set aside time daily to quietly sit with your emotions. Observing your thoughts without judgment can help foster patience and understanding.*
- **Journalling**: *Writing about your grief can be both therapeutic and insightful. It can help track your healing journey and validate your feelings.*
- **Positive Affirmations**: *Reinforce self-compassion with kind, supportive self-talk. Affirmations such as,* "I am grieving at my own pace" *or* "I deserve kindness and care" *can ground you during difficult moments.*
- **Seeking Community**: *Sharing your story with others who understand can provide much-needed comfort and reduce feelings of isolation.*
- **Engaging in Soothing Activities**: *Whether it's walking in nature, reading, meditating, or being creative, find moments of peace that help you reconnect with yourself.*

Grief is a challenging and deeply emotional journey. Approaching it with patience and compassion allows space for true healing. In doing so, you honour your loss, your love, and your resilience.

## Sudden and Accidental Loss:

Navigating the aftermath of a sudden, accidental death—such as from a road accident—is profoundly different from coping with the loss of someone through illness or the natural passing of old age. The suddenness, lack of warning, and often violent nature of such an event can leave loved ones reeling, not only with grief but with overwhelming shock and disbelief.

When a person dies after a long illness or due to old age, there is usually time to prepare emotionally. Though no less painful, these losses often come with opportunities for closure—goodbyes, shared memories, and mutual support among family and friends. There may be a sense of readiness or inevitability, even if the loss remains deeply felt.

By contrast, an accidental death strikes without warning. One moment, life is proceeding as usual; the next, everything has changed irrevocably. There is no time to prepare, no final words shared. The person who was just present—laughing, talking, living—is suddenly gone, leaving behind a disorienting void.

These sudden losses often bring additional emotional burdens. Alongside grief, there may be a powerful sense of injustice, confusion, and anger. Loved ones may think, *"It shouldn't have happened this way."* They may struggle with guilt, asking themselves if something could have been done differently, or become trapped in the randomness of it all.

The trauma of the event itself—especially if the circumstances were violent—can intensify grief and lead to post-traumatic stress. Survivors may be haunted by graphic details, sounds, or mental images that are difficult to escape. This complicates the grieving process, making it harder to process emotions in a healthy way.

Seeking meaning in the face of such senseless loss can be especially difficult. The death of someone young or in the prime of life can feel particularly cruel. Unlike a natural death, there is often no comforting narrative or sense of closure. The absence of answers or explanations can prolong the pain.

Support networks, too, may falter. Friends and family might struggle to know what to say or may avoid the topic altogether, leaving the bereaved feeling isolated and misunderstood.

Healing from an accidental death often requires time and a different approach. Addressing the trauma may involve therapy, group support to connect with others who have experienced similar losses, and personal ways of honouring the memory of the person who has been lost. The journey is often longer and more complex, but with patience and the right support, it is possible to find a way forward, even after such a devastating event. I have met people who have dealt with such grief and here is their story.

## The Story of Lindsay and Peter:

As the couple entered my room, I invited them to take a seat. They greeted me politely and sat down. I explained how I work and that I would share some information first and ask them to respond only with a simple 'yes' or 'no' to confirm whether it was accurate. They seemed so lost I wasn't sure if they had taken in anything I had said. I closed my eyes, and connected with my spirit guide to receive insight into the person they had come to hear from. It didn't take long until I connected with a young soul.

I said, "Your son is here," and told them it was Ethan but I had another name too – Eeps! It was his nickname only they used. They both dissolved in tears before me. I confirmed that Ethan was present with them constantly and he was at peace. I then shared a few of his childhood memories, and they were stunned. These were moments only they could have known about.

Towards the end of the reading, I received the message, 'Ethan didn't get the tattoo,' they both appeared to find this amusing but they received it with a 'yes'. I was puzzled by the information but later was told that he had joked with them before he had left that day that as soon as he was eighteen, he would be getting a tattoo!!! The experience that day left them both shocked and comforted, realising their son had come through and he was actually sending messages and comfort to them.

Lindsay and Peter's life had been like that of any other suburban couple. They had a comfortable home, steady jobs, and their pride and joy: their 17-year-old son, Ethan. He was the light of their lives—a bright, kind-hearted boy with a passion for football and dreams of studying engineering. His future seemed boundless, and they often spoke about the adventures he would embark on after finishing school. But in a single, tragic moment, everything changed.

It was a Saturday evening, and Ethan had gone out with friends, as he often did at weekends. Lindsay and Peter had spent the day running errands, preparing for a quiet night in. They were watching a film when the phone rang. Lindsay answered, expecting it to be Ethan calling to say he'd be home late. Instead, it was a voice she couldn't quite place—calm, detached, and terrifyingly serious. It was a police officer.

*"Mrs Thompson, there's been an accident. Your son, Ethan, has been involved. You need to come to the hospital right away."*

The words hit her like a physical blow. She dropped the phone, her body going cold as panic set in. Peter, alarmed by the look on her face, grabbed the phone and listened as the officer repeated the grim message. Without a word, they were out the door, the film still playing on the television, forgotten.

The drive to the hospital was a blur. Peter gripped the steering wheel so tightly his knuckles turned white, while Lindsay sat in stunned silence, clutching her phone as if it could somehow turn back time. When they arrived at A&E, they were met by a doctor who led them into a quiet room. The look on his face said it all, even before he spoke the words that would shatter their world.

*"Ethan didn't make it,"* the doctor said softly. *"He was involved in a serious road accident. The impact was severe, and despite our best efforts, we couldn't save him. I'm so sorry."*

Lindsay let out a wail that came from the depths of her soul—a sound Peter would never forget. He felt as though he had been punched in the stomach, the air knocked out of him. Everything went numb, and the world seemed to tilt on its axis. They were taken to a room where Ethan lay, lifeless—his body bruised and broken, but his face strangely peaceful. The sight of their son, once so full of life, now gone, was too much to bear. Lindsay collapsed into Peter's arms, her sobs shaking them both to the core.

In the days and weeks that followed, Lindsay and Peter struggled to comprehend what had happened. The funeral came and went—a blur of black clothing, tear-streaked faces, and words of condolence that felt hollow. Their house, once filled with Ethan's laughter and energy, became a silent tomb. His room remained untouched, as if they couldn't bear to admit he was never coming back. The silence was deafening.

The couple, once so close and open with one another, began to drift apart. Lindsay withdrew into herself, spending hours in Ethan's room, clutching his favourite hoodie, surrounded by his belongings, as if she could still feel his presence. Peter, on the other hand, buried himself in work, desperate to escape the crushing grief that awaited him at home. They hardly spoke, each lost in their own world of pain.

At night, Lindsay would lie awake, staring at the ceiling, replaying the night of the accident over and over in her mind. She tormented herself with questions that had no answers. Why hadn't they insisted Ethan stay home that night? Could they have done something—anything—to prevent it? The guilt was unbearable, even though she knew, deep down, that it wasn't her fault.

Peter coped differently. He became consumed with anger—at the driver who had run a red light and hit

Ethan's car, at the universe for taking his son away, and even, irrationally, at himself for not protecting his family. He began to withdraw from everyone, including Lindsay, bottling up his emotions until they threatened to consume him. He couldn't understand why Lindsay seemed stuck in her grief, unable to move forward. He wanted to fix things, to make it better, but there was nothing he could do. He lost his temper often, lashing out at anyone who crossed his path, unable to express the deep and damaging frustration he carried.

Their once-solid marriage began to crack under the strain of their unspoken grief. They argued over small things—whether to leave Ethan's room untouched, what to do with his belongings, even what to have for dinner. But these arguments were merely symptoms of the deeper pain they both carried, a pain they didn't know how to share with each other.

One evening, several months after the accident, Peter came home to find Lindsay sitting on the edge of Ethan's bed, tears streaming down her face. He had witnessed this scene many times before, but something in him finally broke. He sat beside her, his own eyes filling with tears.

*"I miss him so much,"* Lindsay whispered, her voice cracking. *"I don't know how to live without him."*

Peter nodded, his throat too tight to speak. For the first time since the accident, he allowed himself to truly feel the weight of his grief. He wrapped his arms around Lindsay, and they cried together—the walls they had built around their pain finally coming down.

It was at this point that I met them both. We had a few psychic sessions where we connected with Ethan and received messages from him, and he let them know that he was okay, and that he was still with them—present during their times of sadness and grief.

From that moment, they began to heal—slowly, painfully, but together. They learned to talk about their feelings, to support one another rather than retreat into solitude. It wasn't easy, and there were days when the pain felt as fresh as it had on the night of the accident. But they were no longer alone in their grief.

Lindsay and Peter knew they would never fully recover from losing Ethan. The hole he left in their lives would always remain. But they also knew they had to find a way to keep living—to honour Ethan's memory by cherishing the time they had with him, rather than letting his death destroy them. They began to talk about him more openly, sharing stories and memories that made them smile through the tears.

Eventually, they found a new rhythm to life—one that included Ethan's memory as a constant presence, but that also allowed them to move forward. They established a fund in his name at his secondary school, ensuring that his passion for learning would help others achieve their dreams. And, in time, they found a way to live with their grief—together—as they knew Ethan would have wanted.

# Chapter Two

## *The Immediate Aftermath – Breaking the News*

The day my father passed away is etched into my memory with painful clarity. The hours and days that followed were a blur of shock, disbelief, and an overwhelming sense of loss. Navigating the immediate aftermath of his death was one of the most challenging experiences of my life. In this chapter, I will share my journey through those initial days and offer insights and guidance for others facing a similar situation.

The initial shock felt as though the ground had been pulled out from beneath me. My father had always been a constant, steadfast presence in my life, and his sudden passing was incomprehensible. I felt numb, as though I were moving through a fog. Life around me continued as normal, but my reality had shattered. I couldn't eat or sleep for several days, and I barely spoke, except to inform others of what had happened. In many ways, it felt as if I were trapped in a dream—or a film—lacking the energy to play my part. I didn't know how to react or respond to offers of help. It was as though I had lost all sense of reason and could no longer make even the simplest decisions.

Shock can manifest in many different ways. Some people cry uncontrollably, while others, like me, may feel emotionally numb and disconnected. It's important to allow yourself to respond naturally. There is no right or wrong way to grieve such a profound loss.

One of the most difficult tasks in the immediate aftermath was informing family and friends. Every phone call and conversation made the reality of my father's death more tangible. The reactions varied—some were silent, others wept openly, and a few tried to offer words of comfort. It was a painful process, but it also brought moments of connection and shared grief.

When breaking the news to others, it helps to be as clear and direct as possible. The following steps can make the process a little more manageable:

**Prepare Yourself:** Take a moment to gather your thoughts before making each call. Deep breaths can help centre you.

**Be Direct:** Use clear, simple language. Phrases like "Dad passed away this morning" or "I have some sad news about Dad" help convey the message without ambiguity.

**Offer Basic Details:** Provide essential information, such as the date of passing and any immediate plans for services. Save more detailed conversations for later.

**Accept Reactions:** Understand that people will respond differently. Some may offer immediate support; others may need time to process the news.

**Ask for Help:** If making these calls feels too overwhelming, ask a trusted friend or family member to help you share the news.

After informing family and friends, there is often a short period before funeral planning begins. For me, this was the most difficult time. It was strange and disorienting. It felt as if the world had stopped spinning, even though everything around me continued as though nothing had changed. That space was filled with overwhelming grief, logistical concerns, and fleeting moments of connection and support.

During those days, I found comfort in small, familiar routines. I took long walks, allowing the sun to warm my face and the wind to tousle my hair, finding a sense of peace in nature. I spent hours looking through old photographs and reminiscing about the happy times we had shared as a family. These small acts helped me to process my grief, little by little. It was during this time that I began to sense my father's presence around me—guiding me, and in some ways, comforting me. I reflected deeply on who he would have wanted at his funeral, and what I wished to say about him and his life.

Planning my father's funeral felt surreal. I was in a daze, yet decisions had to be made quickly. Fortunately, my family came together to support one another. We discussed my father's wishes and did our best to honour them.

Here are some key steps to consider when making funeral arrangements:

**Gather Important Documents:** Locate your loved one's will, if they had one, as well as any pre-arranged funeral plans or life insurance policies. These can offer guidance and financial support.

**Choose a Funeral Home:** If your loved one hadn't specified one, ask for recommendations or check online reviews. Once selected, the funeral home can guide you through the process.

**Plan the Service:** Decide on the type of service to book whether a traditional funeral, a memorial service, or a celebration of life. Include personal touches that reflect your loved one's character, such as their favourite music or readings.

**Notify Extended Family and Friends:** Make sure extended family members, friends, and colleagues are informed. This can be done via calls, messages, or social media.

**Obituaries and Announcements:** Work with the funeral home to draft and publish an obituary in local newspapers and online. This serves both as a tribute and a public notice.

**Handle Logistics:** Organise transportation, floral arrangements, and any reception plans. Delegate tasks to family and friends to lighten your burden.

My father's funeral was emotionally draining, yet it brought a sense of closure and connection. Seeing so many people who cared for him come together to pay their respects was deeply moving. We shared stories, laughter, and tears as we honoured his life and legacy.

Here are some tips for getting through the day:

**Take Care of Yourself:** Try to rest the night before and eat something, even if you have no appetite. Stay hydrated throughout the day.

**Lean on Support:** Allow yourself to rely on family and friends for emotional support. Don't hesitate to step away for a moment of solitude if needed.

**Participate in the Service:** If you feel comfortable, consider speaking at the service—sharing a memory or reading a tribute can be a meaningful way to honour your loved one.

**Accept Help:** Many people will offer assistance. Accept it—whether they're setting up the venue, preparing food, or simply being there for you.

As the funeral approached, we focused on the final preparations. There were practical matters to attend to—vehicles to arrange, flowers to choose, and a reception to organise. These tasks, while difficult, gave us a sense of purpose and a way to honour my father's memory.

In the days between his death and the funeral, I learned the importance of patience and self-compassion. The grieving and planning process were overwhelming, yet I experienced moments of reflection and support. By leaning on loved ones and taking things step by step, I slowly began to find a way forward—one that honoured my father's life while helping me begin to heal.

The immediate aftermath of losing my father was a whirlwind of emotion and responsibility. Each step—from informing others to planning the funeral—felt insurmountable. Yet, with the support of those around me and a quiet strength I hadn't known I possessed, I managed to navigate that painful chapter.

Remember, there is no "correct" way to grieve, nor is there a timeline for healing. Allow yourself the space to mourn, to remember, and to begin finding your path forward. The love and memories shared with your loved one remain a part of you, guiding you through the days ahead.

In the wake of such a loss, the outpouring of condolences from family, friends, and acquaintances can feel both overwhelming and comforting. Navigating these interactions with grace can provide comfort not only to yourself but also to those who wish to offer support.

When people extend their condolences, they are reaching out to share your sorrow and show their support. Even when words may seem inadequate, it's important to appreciate the kindness behind them.

**Acknowledge Their Effort:** A simple "Thank you for your kind words" can go a long way in recognising someone's support.

**Allow Yourself to Feel:** Let their words affect you. It's okay to be emotional. Genuine reactions often deepen the sense of connection.

**Be Present:** Try to stay present in the moment when receiving condolences. Listening attentively and responding thoughtfully shows appreciation for their support.

Responding to condolences can be difficult, especially when you're emotionally overwhelmed. Keeping your responses simple and sincere is perfectly acceptable.

**Express Gratitude:** Phrases like "Thank you for your sympathy" or "Your support means a great deal to me" are heartfelt and sufficient.

**Share Briefly:** If you feel comfortable, share a short memory or sentiment about your loved one. This can make the exchange more personal and meaningful. For example: *"Dad always enjoyed your company at our family gatherings. He spoke of you often."*

**Allow for Silence:** Sometimes, words aren't necessary. A hug, a nod, or a shared moment of silence can speak volumes and offer comfort.

There may be times when the influx of condolences feels overwhelming. It's important to take care of yourself during these interactions.

**Set Boundaries:** If you need a moment alone, it's perfectly acceptable to excuse yourself politely. For example: *"Thank you for your kind words. I need a moment to myself right now, but I appreciate your support."*

**Lean on a Support System:** Having a close friend or family member nearby to help manage interactions can be incredibly helpful. They can step in when you need a break or assist in welcoming guests.

**Take Breaks:** Give yourself permission to step away from the crowd and gather your thoughts. Finding a quiet space to breathe and reflect can help you maintain your composure.

People express condolences in different ways—through words, gestures, or actions. Each form of support holds value and can make meaningful contributions to your healing journey.

**Written Condolences:** You can read cards, letters, and emails at your own pace. They offer comfort when you're ready. Keep them in a special place to revisit whenever you need a reminder of the support surrounding you.

**Gestures of Kindness:** Acts such as bringing food, offering to run errands, or simply being present are tangible demonstrations of care. Accept these gestures graciously, recognising the thoughtfulness and love behind them.

**Emotional Support:** Some friends might not know what to say, but their presence alone can be deeply comforting. Sitting together in silence or having a companion for a walk can bring immense solace.

Receiving condolences can also offer an opportunity to reflect on the positive impact your loved one had on others. The stories and memories shared by those offering sympathy may become sources of strength and even joy.

**Collect Memories:** Consider creating a memory book to compile the stories and sentiments shared by others. It can become a treasured keepsake that honours your loved one's legacy.

**Find Strength in Community:** Acknowledge the community supporting you during this time. The collective care and solidarity can be a powerful reminder that you are not alone in your grief.

**Express Thanks:** When you feel ready, consider sending thank-you notes to those who offered condolences. It doesn't have to be immediate; take your time and express your gratitude in a way that feels right to you.

Receiving condolences with grace is not about putting on a brave face—it's about acknowledging and appreciating the kindness extended to you during a profoundly difficult time. By allowing yourself to be present, accepting support, and leaning on your loved ones, you can navigate these interactions with both grace and gratitude. Remember, it's okay to show vulnerability and let others be there for you. Their support may become a vital lifeline as you move through your grief.

Breaking the news of my dad's passing to our extended family was one of the hardest things I've ever had to do. It was a task laden with sorrow and a deep sense of responsibility, knowing my words would carry the weight of our collective loss.

I remember taking a deep breath and grounding myself in a quiet moment of reflection. I wanted to approach this painful duty with the same grace and compassion my dad had always shown in difficult times. He had a remarkable ability to find light even in the darkest moments, and I wanted to honour that spirit.

I began with a call to my aunt, Dad's older sister. Her voice was warm and familiar, filled with echoes of laughter and countless family memories. As I spoke, I chose my words carefully, aiming to convey not only the sadness of his passing but also the peace he had found in his final moments.

"Aunty, I have some very difficult news. Dad passed away peacefully yesterday. He was surrounded by love and warmth, and he was not in pain. I know how much he meant to all of us, and I wanted to share this with you personally."

There was a moment of silence—a heartbeat where the world seemed to pause. Then came a quiet sob. "Oh, sweetheart," she whispered, her voice breaking. "I'm so sorry. He was such a wonderful man."

We spoke for a while, sharing memories and comforting each other. I told her about the signs I had felt, the music we played in his room that seemed to carry his spirit, and how those small moments brought me comfort. She listened, her tears mingling with laughter as we recalled the joy he had brought into our lives.

Next, I called my uncle. His initial reaction was more reserved, but as I delivered the news, I could feel the layers of his grief unfold.

"He was my best friend," he said, his voice cracking. "I can't believe he's gone."

"I know," I replied. "It's hard to accept. But I feel him with us—in the music he loved and in the memories we share. He's still here, watching over us."

Breaking the news continued with more calls, each one a delicate thread woven into the tapestry of our family's mourning. With every conversation, I tried to convey not just the sorrow of our loss, but also the enduring legacy of love and connection Dad had left behind.

In the days that followed, we found solace in one another. We shared stories, laughter, and tears—drawing strength from the love Dad had nurtured in us. Through these conversations, I came to realise that informing others of his passing was not only a duty, but also a means of uniting us in grief and honouring his memory together.

In those moments of shared sorrow and remembrance, I felt Dad's presence more strongly than ever. He was there in the laughter that broke through the tears, in the comforting words exchanged, and in the music that seemed to play just when we needed it most. His spirit—warm, gentle, and full of light—continued to guide us through the darkness, reminding us that love transcends even the deepest loss.

After the funeral concluded, a deep sense of emptiness settled over me, mingled with a bittersweet relief that his suffering had ended. The house—once filled with his laughter and the rhythm of his daily life—now echoed with silence. Friends and family, who had gathered to offer support and share memories, gradually departed, leaving behind an overwhelming quiet.

Yet, amidst the solitude, I found comfort in the memories we had shared and a renewed determination to honour his legacy by living the values he had taught us. The journey of grief had only just begun, but so had the slow, gentle process of healing and remembrance.

Here is a light-hearted story of validation that brought comfort to a woman named Sarah after she came to see me:

When Sarah came for a reading, she was hoping to connect with her Grandma Betty, who had passed away the previous year. Grandma Betty was famous in the family for her cooking—especially her apple pies, which were the highlight of every family gathering. Sarah missed those pies almost as much as she missed her grandma.

As soon as we began, I felt Grandma Betty's warm presence.

"Your grandma is here," I told Sarah. "She's showing me a kitchen, and there's a wonderful smell of baking."

Sarah smiled, her eyes misting over. "That sounds like her. She was always in the kitchen, making something delicious."

I focused on the details Grandma Betty was sharing.

"She's very particular about her apple pie. She's showing me a memory of you two baking together. But she's laughing—something about a secret ingredient."

Sarah's face lit up with recognition. "Oh no, not the secret ingredient! We never could figure out what made her pies so special."

I grinned, the image becoming clearer.

"Well, she's letting me in on the secret now. It seems that one day, while you were busy peeling apples, she added a splash of... whiskey to the pie filling!"

Sarah gasped, then burst out laughing. "Whiskey? Are you serious? She always called it 'Grandma's magic touch' but never mentioned whiskey!"

I laughed too.

"She's saying she used to sneak it in when no one was looking—just a little bit, for that extra warmth and flavour. She found it hilarious that no one ever guessed."

Sarah shook her head, still laughing. "That's so her! She loved little secrets and surprises. And it makes perfect sense now—her pies always had this special kick that we couldn't replicate."

Grandma Betty's spirit was clearly enjoying the moment. She had one more thing to share:

"She says she loved those times with you in the kitchen—and that the real secret ingredient was the love and laughter you shared."

Sarah's laughter softened into a warm smile. "Thank you. This is exactly what I needed to hear. It's such a perfect reminder of her."

As the reading concluded, we both felt a deep sense of connection and joy. Grandma Betty had not only validated her presence through the funny and unexpected revelation of her secret ingredient, but she had also reaffirmed the enduring love that continues to bind her and Sarah together.

# Chapter Three

## *Emotional Rollercoaster – After the Funeral*

The funeral was over, and the last of the guests had departed. The house, once bustling with activity and filled with the comforting hum of conversation, now felt eerily quiet. I stood in the living room, surrounded by the remnants of a week marked by grief, support, and shared memories. The silence was deafening, amplifying the void left by my father's absence.

As I sank into my father's favourite chair, the weight of the past few days began to settle on me. The emotional rollercoaster had been relentless, and I felt caught in a whirlwind of grief, relief, guilt, and longing. Each wave of emotion crashed over me, pulling me under before pushing me back to the surface—only for the cycle to repeat.

Grief became my constant companion. It struck unexpectedly—a lingering whiff of his cologne in the hallway, the sight of his untouched reading glasses on the coffee table, or a photograph capturing him laughing at a family gathering. Each reminder was like a dagger to the heart, a stark symbol of the permanence of his absence.

Relief was an emotion I struggled to accept. It was intricately entwined with guilt, forming a painful knot in my chest. My father had suffered for a long time, and there was comfort in knowing that his pain had ended. Yet that relief felt like a betrayal, as though feeling anything but sorrow was like being disloyal to his memory. I questioned myself constantly—was it wrong to feel relieved? Did it mean I loved him any less?

Guilt was pervasive, creeping into my thoughts and magnifying every decision I had made. I replayed our final conversations, wondering whether I had said everything I needed to, whether I had done enough to ease his last days. The guilt was relentless, whispering that I should have done more, been more. Every time I smiled or laughed, it felt like the worst kind of betrayal—wasn't I supposed to be grieving?

Longing settled deep within me, a constant ache for what had been lost. I longed for one more conversation, one more piece of advice, one more opportunity to tell him how much he meant to me. The finality of death made these longings feel simultaneously trivial and monumental. Every missed opportunity felt like a wound that would never fully heal.

As the days turned into weeks, I navigated the emotional landscape with varying degrees of success. Some days brought moments of peace—brief interludes where the pain softened and I could remember my father with a smile instead of tears. Other days, the sorrow was all-consuming, leaving me adrift in a sea of sadness.

One evening, I sat with my mother looking through old family photographs. We came across an album filled with pictures of my father in his youth. There he was—vibrant and full of life—a stark contrast to the frail figure he had become in his final days. As I turned each page, I felt a subtle shift within me. The photos told the story of a life well lived: of love, adventure, and resilience. They reminded me that my father was more than his final days, more than his suffering.

These photographs became a way to reconnect with his legacy and find solace in his memory. Gradually, I began to see this emotional rollercoaster as a journey—one that would eventually lead me toward acceptance and healing. The highs and lows were part of the process, each wave of emotion a step closer to understanding and embracing my new reality.

In the weeks and months that followed, I learned to navigate my grief with greater compassion for myself. I allowed myself to feel every emotion without judgement, understanding that they were all part of the complex tapestry of loss. I found comfort in the things my father had loved—his favourite music, cherished books, and well-loved TV shows. These small acts of remembrance became bridges between the past and the present, helping me carry his memory forward in a meaningful way.

Grief is a journey without a clear destination. It winds through valleys of sorrow and peaks of bittersweet joy, a testament to the depth of our love and the weight of our loss. As I continued down this path, I found strength in the knowledge that my father's legacy lived on within me—in the values he instilled, the lessons he taught, and the love he gave. And in that, I found a measure of peace amidst the turbulence.

During this time, I found myself increasingly drawn to spiritualism and the comfort it offered. I often felt my father's presence and could hear his guiding words more clearly, helping me move forward and aiding my decisions in moments when I still felt deeply alone.

Spiritualism and death are profoundly intertwined, offering a framework through which individuals seek meaning and solace in the face of mortality. Spiritualism holds that death is not an end but a transition—a passage into another realm where the soul continues its journey. This belief offers great comfort, suggesting that loved ones are not lost but transformed, maintaining a presence that can still be felt and even communicated with through spiritual practices. It emphasises the continuity of life, the persistence of the spirit, and the interconnectedness of all beings, fostering a sense of peace and acceptance in the face of death's inevitability. For those who embrace spiritualism, death becomes a gateway to deeper understanding and a reminder of the enduring nature of the soul.

In the days and weeks following your loved one's funeral, finding practical ways to move forward can offer structure and support as you navigate your grief. Here are some steps that may help:

**Establish a Routine:** Create a daily schedule to restore a sense of stability. This can include simple tasks such as waking at the same time each day, maintaining regular meals, and incorporating gentle exercise or meditation.

**Seek Support:** Reach out to friends, family, or support groups. Sharing your feelings and memories can be comforting and help you feel less isolated. Qualified counselling or grief therapy can also be invaluable.

**Handle Administrative Tasks:** Take care of essential responsibilities such as notifying institutions, managing your loved one's estate, and addressing legal matters. Break these into manageable steps, and seek help if you feel overwhelmed.

**Create a Memory Box:** Collect photographs, letters, and personal items that remind you of your loved one. A memory box can serve as a tangible way to honour their legacy and feel close to them.

**Engage in Activities:** Participate in hobbies or activities that you or your loved one enjoyed. This can be a way to pay tribute to them while offering you a constructive outlet for grief. Volunteering or joining a local group can also provide a sense of purpose and connection.

**Take Care of Yourself:** Prioritise self-care by eating healthy, getting enough sleep, and engaging in physical activity. Grief affects the body as well as the mind, so it's essential to look after your overall well-being.

**Set Small Goals:** Establishing and achieving small, manageable goals can help restore a sense of control and accomplishment—whether related to work, household tasks, or personal projects.

**Allow Yourself to Grieve:** Permit yourself to feel all emotions without guilt. Grief is highly individual, and there's no 'right' way to experience it. Take time to cry, remember, and honour your loved one in ways that feel meaningful to you.

**Seek Professional Help If Needed:** If grief becomes overwhelming or begins to interfere with daily life, consider speaking with a mental health practitioner who specialises in bereavement.

**Plan Memorial Activities:** Ongoing rituals such as planting a tree, holding an annual remembrance ceremony, or supporting a cause your loved one cared about can provide enduring ways to honour their memory.

It's also important to allow yourself moments of happiness, even as you grieve. Grief is layered and complex, and experiencing joy does not lessen the depth of your sorrow or diminish the love you feel. Embracing small moments of joy can provide relief and restore balance. Whether it's laughter shared with a friend, comfort found in a favourite hobby, or the quiet warmth of a cherished memory, these moments are not betrayals—they are affirmations of life and love. They remind us that it's okay to live fully, even while mourning. Allowing happiness into your life is a vital part of healing, honouring both the memory of your loved one and your continued journey forward.

Moving forward after your loved one's funeral is a gradual process, blending practical tasks with emotional healing. By attending to necessary matters, seeking support, and finding meaningful ways to honour their memory, you can begin to navigate this difficult time and slowly move towards healing.

## After my father's funeral:

A few days after the funeral, I found myself sitting in Dad's favourite armchair, wrapped in one of his old sweaters that my mother had given me for comfort. I had turned on the radio absentmindedly—more for background noise than anything else. Suddenly, the opening notes of Johnny Mathis's *Chances Are* filled the room. It had been one of Dad's favourite songs; he used to sing it around the house, his voice always brimming with warmth and joy.

Hearing that song felt like a direct message from him. It was such a rare track to hear on the radio, and the timing felt too perfect to be mere coincidence. As the melody played, I was overcome with a strange yet comforting sense of his presence, as though he were there, singing along with me. Tears welled up in my eyes, but for the first time since his passing, they were tears of bittersweet joy rather than pure sorrow.

A few days later, I was sorting through some of Dad's old belongings, trying to bring some order to the chaos. I discovered his collection of vinyl records and decided to play a few of his favourites. As I gently placed the needle on a record, Tina Turner's powerful voice filled the room, singing *Simply the Best*. Dad had always said that song reminded him of my mum and how he felt about our family. Listening to it now, I felt as though he was reminding me of the love and strength he believed in.

Later that week, another sign came in the most unexpected way. I was walking through the park, lost in thought, when I almost failed to notice a street musician setting up near one of the benches. As I approached, he began to play Johnny Mathis's *Misty*, another one of Dad's all-time favourites. The musician's rendition was hauntingly beautiful, and in that moment, it felt as though Dad was serenading me through him—gently reminding me that he was still nearby.

# Chapter Four

## *Physical and Mental Health – Be Kind to Yourself*

The day my father passed away marked a profound shift in my life. The man who had been my anchor, my guide, and my source of strength was suddenly gone, leaving behind a void that felt insurmountable. The impact of his loss echoed through every aspect of my being, affecting both my physical and mental health in ways I could never have foreseen.

In the immediate aftermath, shock and disbelief clouded my mind. I drifted through the days in a daze, mechanically completing necessary tasks while feeling disconnected from reality. The weight of grief bore down on me, making each step feel heavy and burdensome. Sleep became elusive as my mind raced with memories of my father and the painful realisation that he was no longer there. Nights stretched on endlessly, and I often found myself staring at the ceiling, tears streaming down my face as I grappled with the enormity of my loss.

My appetite was one of the first casualties of grief. Food lost all appeal, and the simple act of eating felt like an insurmountable effort. I picked at meals without interest, more out of obligation than desire. The weight began to drop, and friends and family expressed concern, but their words barely registered. It was as if my body had entered survival mode, shutting down anything non-essential to merely existing.

Physically, I felt drained and utterly exhausted. The constant emotional strain manifested as relentless fatigue that no amount of rest could relieve. My muscles ached, and even basic tasks like getting out of bed or taking a shower required immense effort. I suffered frequent headaches and a persistent tightness in my chest, as if my body was mirroring the pain in my heart. My immune system weakened, and I became more susceptible to illness—each cold or flu a reminder of how vulnerable I had become.

The psychological toll of losing my father was even more profound. He had always been my confidant—the person I turned to for advice, reassurance, and perspective. Without him, I felt adrift in a sea of sorrow and uncertainty. Waves of depression crashed over me, leaving me numb and detached from the world. It was difficult to find joy in anything; activities that once brought pleasure now felt hollow and meaningless.

Anxiety became a constant companion. I worried incessantly about the future and my ability to cope without my father's guidance. Every decision, no matter how minor, felt overwhelming. I doubted myself at every turn, second-guessing my choices and fearing I would never live up to his expectations. Panic attacks struck without warning, leaving me gasping for breath and trembling with fear.

Social interactions became increasingly difficult. I withdrew from friends and family, isolating myself in an attempt to shield others from my pain. Conversations felt forced, and I often found myself zoning out, unable to focus on what others were saying. I avoided gatherings and events, afraid I would break down in public or be met with well-meaning but painful questions about my father's death.

Grief also impaired my cognitive function. My concentration was shattered, and even simple tasks at work or home became overwhelming. I would start a project only to abandon it midway, unable to recall why it mattered. My memory suffered—important dates and details slipped through the cracks—fueling my anxiety and deepening my sense of inadequacy. It felt as though my mind was engulfed in a thick fog, obscuring my ability to think clearly and make sound decisions.

Despite the overwhelming nature of my grief, I eventually recognised the importance of seeking help. Friends and family gently encouraged me to speak with a therapist. Though I was initially hesitant, I ultimately agreed. Talking to a professional provided a safe space to explore my emotions and I began to process the loss. Through therapy, I learned it was okay to grieve in my own way and that healing would take time.

I also began to engage in self-care practices, even when they felt like monumental tasks. I forced myself to eat regular meals, starting with small portions of nutritious food that were easier to manage. I began taking short walks, finding solace in the rhythm of my footsteps and the fresh air. Although challenging at first, exercise gradually eased the physical tension and fatigue. I also practised mindfulness and meditation, which offered moments of peace amidst the chaos of my thoughts.

Reconnecting with my father's memory in positive ways became an essential part of my healing journey. I created a scrapbook filled with photographs, letters, and mementoes that captured our time together. Revisiting these memories was bittersweet but also reminded me of the love and joy we had shared. I found comfort in continuing traditions he had cherished—his Saturday morning full English breakfast ritual, or tending to his beloved garden. These activities helped me feel close to him and kept his spirit alive in my everyday life.

Over time, the acute pain of my loss began to soften, though it never completely disappeared. I learned to carry my grief with me, integrating it into my life rather than allowing it to define me. The support of loved ones, the guidance of my therapist, and my own efforts to care for myself all contributed to my gradual healing.

Losing my father had a profound impact on my physical and mental health, shaking me to my core and challenging me in ways I never anticipated. The journey through grief was long and arduous, marked by moments of deep sorrow and fragile hope. Yet through this experience, I discovered a resilience I hadn't known existed. I came to understand that while the pain of loss may never fully fade, it is possible to move forward—to honour the memory of a loved one while continuing to live a life filled with meaning and love.

## Understanding Grief and Its Effects on Health

Losing a loved one is one of the most profound and challenging experiences a person can endure. The grief that follows can deeply affect both physical and mental health. Understanding these impacts and learning how to navigate them is essential to the healing process and finding a way forward.

In the immediate aftermath of a loss, the shock and emotional upheaval can place immense strain on the body. Many experience severe fatigue, as the constant emotional stress leaves them feeling utterly drained. Sleep disturbances are common, making it difficult to fall asleep, stay asleep, or feel rested—even after a full night's rest. This disruption to the sleep cycle can lead to chronic exhaustion, impairing daily function and overall wellbeing.

Grief also affects appetite. Some may lose interest in food entirely, while others might overeat as a means of emotional coping. Both extremes can result in nutritional imbalances that negatively affect physical health. It's important to try and maintain a balanced diet, even when food seems unappealing. Eating small, frequent meals that are easy to prepare and rich in nutrients can help sustain energy levels. Staying hydrated is equally important; grief can be dehydrating, so drinking plenty of water is essential. Additionally, grief can weaken the immune system, making individuals more prone to illness. It is not uncommon for bereaved people to catch colds or infections more frequently.

Mentally, the burden of losing a loved one can be overwhelming. The emotional pain often leads to depression and anxiety. Feelings of loneliness, sadness, and hopelessness are natural, but they can also be debilitating. One of the most vital steps in coping with mental health challenges during grief is acknowledging them. Suppressing or denying emotions can lead to more serious psychological issues in the long run. It is important to allow yourself to feel the full spectrum of your emotions—pain, sadness, anger, confusion. Grieve in the way that feels right for you.

Daily tasks may become difficult to manage, and many people withdraw socially, avoiding friends and family.

This isolation can intensify feelings of despair. Though socialising may feel daunting, maintaining some level of connection with others is important for emotional support.

Exercise, even in its gentlest forms, can be a powerful aid in healing. Though it may feel like the last thing you want to do, physical activity can significantly benefit both your body and mind. It helps reduce stress, lift mood, and increase energy levels. It doesn't need to be strenuous—a short walk, light stretching, or a few minutes of yoga can have a positive impact. Exercise releases endorphins—natural mood enhancers—and helps relieve the physical tension associated with grief. Making a small, consistent effort to move your body each day can gradually support both physical recovery and emotional healing.

## The Grieving Process and Cognitive Impacts

The grieving process can also bring about a range of cognitive changes. You may find it difficult to concentrate, recall information, or make decisions. This mental fog, often referred to as "grief brain," can make it challenging to navigate even simple daily activities.

Dealing with grief fog begins with acknowledging and accepting it as a normal part of the grieving journey. Understand that your brain is under significant stress, and it is entirely natural to experience these difficulties. Attempting to power through or ignore these symptoms may only lead to further frustration and emotional strain.

To manage grief fog, begin by simplifying your daily routines. Break tasks into smaller, more manageable steps and prioritise what truly needs attention. Using lists can be incredibly helpful—write down daily tasks, appointments, and reminders to stay on track. A planner or digital calendar can serve as a visual aid to help you stay organised and ensure that important matters are not overlooked.

Establishing a structured daily routine can also provide a sense of stability and normalcy. Set consistent times for waking up, meals, and activities to create a predictable rhythm in your day. This structure can help ease some of the confusion and disorientation that grief often brings.

Mindfulness and meditation practices can also help to manage the symptoms of grief fog. These practices encourage you to focus on the present moment, which can enhance concentration and reduce mental clutter. Simple breathing exercises or guided meditations can offer moments of clarity and calm, helping to lift the fog and centre your thoughts.

It is important to extend grace and patience to yourself during this time. Grief fog may leave you feeling less productive or capable, but it is vital to remember that these symptoms are temporary and a natural part of the grieving process. Allow yourself the space to rest and take breaks when needed. Overloading yourself with tasks or high expectations can exacerbate cognitive difficulties and increase stress.

Coping with loss involves caring for both body and mind. Your physical well-being can be strengthened through simple acts—resting when you need to, nourishing yourself with wholesome food, and moving your body in ways that feel gentle yet grounding. A slow walk, a stretch, or time outdoors can ease tension and remind you that you are still connected to the rhythms of life.

Emotional care often begins with being heard. Whether it's a quiet conversation over tea, an honest exchange with a friend, or the support of a counsellor, sharing your inner world can lift the weight of isolation. If speaking to those close to you feels daunting, groups for people who have faced similar losses can offer understanding without the need for explanation.

Personal rituals can also bring comfort. You might light a candle at the same time each evening, or engage in creative work that gives form to your feelings. These acts don't have to be grand; what matters is that they reflect your truth in this moment.

Keeping their memory alive can be part of the healing. Curating a small collection of photographs, or quietly continuing a tradition they cherished can serve as a bridge between your life now and the love you still hold.

While life will never be the same after losing someone close, discovering a "new normal" is an essential step in the healing journey. This means adjusting to life without them while gradually embracing new routines and finding sources of joy. It's okay to smile, laugh, and find happiness again. Your loved one would want you to live a full and meaningful life.

Finding ways to remain connected to your loved one can also be comforting—whether it's visiting their resting place, speaking to them in your thoughts, or continuing a cherished tradition. Some people find solace in writing letters to their departed loved one, expressing feelings and thoughts as though they were still present.

Let's look at Emma's journey of grief that she shared with me when I met her.

## Emma's Journey

Emma walked into my office for a psychic reading. As she settled into the chair, the exhaustion etched into her face was immediately evident.

"I don't know how to move forward," she whispered, her voice trembling. "I feel lost, and I don't know how to find my way back to living."

We began the session with a moment of quiet reflection, inviting Emma's loved one's presence into the room. Almost instantly, I felt a warm, gentle energy, like the soft embrace of a summer breeze. I shared this with Emma, and tears welled up in her eyes.

“Lizzy is here,” I said softly. “She wants you to know that she’s always with you, watching over you with love.”

Emma looked shocked at my words. She had never told me it was her daughter who had passed and her name was Lizzy. Emma’s tears flowed freely, there was a mixture of relief and longing on her face. “I miss her so much. Every day is a struggle. I can’t sleep, I can’t eat, and I can’t find joy in anything.”

Throughout the reading, Lizzy conveyed messages filled with love and reassurance. She spoke of the beautiful memories they had shared and encouraged Emma to hold onto those joyful moments. She reminded her mother of their shared love for gardening, urging her to return to the garden they had once tended together.

“Lizzy says that spending time in the garden will help you feel close to her,” I relayed. “She wants you to plant new flowers—ones that remind you of her. Each bloom will be a sign of her presence, a reminder that life continues, and that beauty still exists.”

Emma nodded, a small smile breaking through her tears. "Lizzy always loved the garden. She would spend hours picking flowers and making little bouquets."

As the session progressed, we also discussed the toll the loss had taken on Emma's physical and emotional well-being. Lizzy's message was clear: it was time for Emma to take care of herself and allow healing to begin. She encouraged her mother to seek support from loved ones and not to isolate herself in her grief.

"Lizzy wants you to know that it's okay to ask for help," I said. "She knows how strong you are, but she also knows you don't have to carry this burden alone."

Emma took a deep breath, taking in her daughter's words. "I've been trying to be strong for so long," she admitted. "But I see now that I need to look after myself too."

After each reading, I always check in with my clients to ensure they feel more at ease before they leave. I later learned that the loss of her daughter, Lizzy, had cast a long shadow over Emma's life. She had come to me seeking a spiritual connection—hoping to find some comfort and a sense of closeness to her beloved child.

The preceding months had taken a severe toll on her. Her once-vibrant eyes were dulled by sleepless nights, and she had lost a noticeable amount of weight—her appetite diminished by the persistent sorrow that enveloped her daily life.

In the weeks that followed, Emma began making small yet meaningful changes. She reached out to friends and family, allowing herself to be supported. She returned to the garden, planting flowers in Lizzy's memory. Each new bloom brought her a sense of peace and connection to her daughter.

She also sought professional help and began working through her grief with a therapist. Gradually, the physical symptoms of her sorrow began to ease. Her appetite returned, and her sleep improved. The burden of grief still remained—but it no longer felt as suffocating.

Emma continued to visit me for readings, each time discovering greater strength and resilience within herself. Lizzy's presence remained a guiding light, helping her mother navigate the darkness of loss. Through these sessions, Emma found renewed purpose and a way to honour her daughter's memory while also caring for herself.

The journey of healing was long and often difficult, but with each step, Emma moved closer to a place of peace. She came to understand that while the pain of losing Lizzy would never fully disappear, she could live with it—and even rediscover moments of beauty and joy.

# Chapter Five

## *The Role of Support Systems – Reaching Out*

### Navigating the Journey of Grief: Asking for and Accepting Support

In overwhelming grief, support systems become invaluable. However, many people struggle with knowing how to ask for help and how to accept it when offered. This chapter explores the importance of support systems, how to reach out for assistance, and how to graciously receive the help that comes your way.

Support systems offer emotional comfort, practical assistance, and a sense of connection during a time when you feel isolated and adrift. Friends, family, colleagues, and support groups can all form a network that helps you navigate complex emotions and logistical challenges of losing a loved one. These systems remind you that you are not alone and provide a sense of stability amidst the chaos of grief.

Emotional support is perhaps the most significant benefit of a strong support system. Sharing your feelings with those who care about you can offer immense relief. It allows you to express sorrow, anger, confusion, and even fleeting moments of joy without fear of judgement. These conversations validate your emotions and help you process your loss more effectively.

Practical support is equally important. Grief can make even the simplest tasks feel daunting. Friends and family can assist with everyday activities such as cooking, cleaning, or running errands. This kind of help can alleviate some of the burden, allowing you to focus on emotional healing.

Asking for help can be difficult, especially if you are used to being independent. It is common to feel hesitant, fearing that you might burden others or appear weak. However, reaching out for support is a sign of strength, not weakness. Here are some steps to help you ask for help effectively:

**Identify Your Needs:** Take time to understand what you require. Is it emotional support, someone to talk to, or practical help with daily tasks? Clarifying your needs makes it easier to communicate them to others.

**Choose the Right People:** Consider who in your network is best suited to assist with specific needs. Friends, family members, and colleagues may all offer different forms of support. Some may be great listeners, while others are more practical helpers.

**Be Specific:** When asking for help, be clear and precise. Instead of saying, "I need help," try, "Could you come over and help me with dinner?" or "Can we talk? I really need someone to listen."

**Express Your Feelings:** Let the person know how you're feeling and that their support would mean a lot. This fosters empathy and deeper connection.

**Be Honest:** It is okay to admit that you're struggling. Being open about your feelings and needs can strengthen relationships and enable others to support you more effectively.

Receiving help can be just as challenging as asking for it. Many people feel uncomfortable accepting assistance due to pride, guilt, or the belief that they should cope alone. Here are some strategies to help you receive help graciously:

**Acknowledge Your Limits:** Recognise that it's okay not to have everything under control. Grief can deplete your energy and make daily tasks difficult. Accepting help is an act of self-care.

**Practise Gratitude:** When someone offers help, show appreciation. A simple "thank you" can go a long way. Expressing gratitude not only makes the giver feel valued but also helps you accept the support being offered.

**Let Go of Guilt:** Accepting help does not mean you are a burden. Most people want to help and feel good about being there for you. Release any guilt and allow yourself to receive kindness with an open heart.

**Be Open:** Try to remain open to various forms of support. Even if the assistance offered isn't exactly what you had in mind, it may still be helpful. Flexibility can make the support more meaningful.

**Communicate:** If the help offered isn't quite what you need, it's okay to say so. Be clear and respectful in communicating your preferences. Most people will appreciate being guided in how to best support you.

**Set Boundaries:** It's important to set limits if you feel overwhelmed. Let others know when you need space or time alone. Balancing external support with personal time is essential to your well-being.

Building a support network involves cultivating relationships that are mutually supportive. Here are some ways to build and maintain such a network:

**Reach Out Regularly:** Keep in touch with friends and family, even if it's just through a quick message or call. Regular communication strengthens relationships and makes it easier to seek help when needed.

**Be There for Others:** Support is a two-way street. Offer your help when others are in need. Being present for loved ones builds reciprocal relationships that can sustain you during difficult times.

**Join Support Groups:** Consider attending a grief support group. These communities can offer shared understanding and comfort. Connecting with others who have experienced similar losses can be incredibly healing.

**Seek Professional Help:** Therapists and counsellors can play an essential role in your support system. They provide expert perspective and guidance, helping you navigate the complexities of grief.

**Nurture Your Relationships:** Invest in maintaining strong and healthy connections. Show appreciation for the support you receive and remain mindful of the needs of others. Strong relationships are built on mutual respect and care.

In addition to emotional and practical support, spiritual support can be a powerful source of comfort during times of grief. For many, spirituality offers a sense of peace, hope, and connection to something greater than themselves. Whether through religious practices, personal faith, or spiritual beliefs, this form of support can help bring meaning and acceptance to your experience of loss.

Spiritual practices such as prayer, meditation, and attending religious services can provide moments of reflection and solace. These rituals can help you feel closer to your loved one and bring a sense of continuity and purpose. Whether part of a formal tradition or uniquely personal, these practices can honour your loved one's memory and provide comfort.

Seeking guidance from a spiritual advisor—such as a pastor, priest, rabbi, imam, or spiritual counsellor—can also be beneficial. These individuals offer wisdom, support, and a compassionate ear. They can help you explore your feelings, find meaning in your loss, and reassure you that your loved one's spirit lives on in some way.

Spending time in nature can also provide a spiritual connection. Many feel a grounding peace in the natural world—through walking in the park, hiking, or simply sitting quietly in a garden. Nature's beauty and stillness can offer a powerful reminder of life's cycles and the continuing presence of your loved one in the world around you.

Incorporating spiritual practices into your daily routine can help you find moments of peace and meaning. This might include setting aside quiet time for reflection, lighting a candle in your loved one's memory, or reading spiritual texts that offer comfort. These rituals can anchor you during turbulent times and support emotional healing.

In conclusion, navigating the loss of a loved one is profoundly challenging, but a robust support system can make a significant difference. By learning to ask for and accept help, you create a network that sustains you through the darkest moments. Remember, needing support does not make you weak. On the contrary, accepting help strengthens your resilience and nurtures your capacity to heal. Here's a story that shows support comes in many forms, even in meals.

## Claire's Story – A Mountain of Meals and a Lesson in Friendship

When Claire lost her beloved mother, she was plunged into a sea of grief that felt endless. In those early days, she could barely muster the energy to get out of bed, let alone prepare a meal. Her best friend, Emma, full of well-meaning enthusiasm, decided that Claire should never have to worry about food during this difficult time. Emma's intentions were pure, but what followed became a story that Claire now recalls with laughter and affection.

Emma had always expressed care through action—especially culinary action. She loved to cook and saw it as her personal mission to ensure Claire was well-fed. On the day of the funeral, Emma arrived with a casserole dish. The following day, it was a pot of soup. By the end of the week, Claire's fridge was packed to capacity with all the food Emma had brought her.

At first, Claire was deeply grateful. The meals were delicious and saved her from the daunting task of cooking. But as the days turned into weeks, the flow of food from Emma grew into a flood. Each visit brought another dish—lasagne, chicken pie, shepherd's pie, and more casseroles than Claire could count. Her kitchen counters became a buffet of Tupperware containers and foil-covered trays.

Claire didn't want to hurt Emma's feelings by telling her she was overwhelmed by the sheer volume of food. She also didn't have the heart to admit that she was running out of storage space and had even resorted to stashing some meals in her neighbour's freezer. Whenever Emma asked how she was doing, Claire would plaster on a smile and say, "I'm managing, thank you so much for the food!"

One day, Claire's other friend, Sarah, came over for a visit. Sarah took one look at the kitchen and burst out laughing.

"Claire, this looks like a catering service! Are you running a secret restaurant out of your home?"

Claire couldn't help but laugh too. "I know! Emma has been so generous, but I don't know how to tell her that I just can't eat all of this food. I don't want to hurt her feelings. She's only trying to help."

Sarah, ever the practical one, suggested, "Why don't we throw a party? We can invite some friends over to help eat the food. It'll lift your spirits and clear some space in your fridge."

The idea of a party was exactly what Claire needed. They called a few friends, and soon a small gathering was underway in Claire's living room. The party was a hit, and Claire's friends were more than happy to help her eat through what they jokingly called *Emma's mountain of meals*. Everyone had a wonderful time, and for the first time in weeks, Claire found herself laughing and truly enjoying the company of her friends.

When Emma arrived and saw the party, she was initially surprised but quickly joined in the fun. Claire finally had the chance to explain.

"Emma, your meals have been a lifeline, but I couldn't keep up with how much there was! I didn't know how to tell you without sounding ungrateful."

Emma laughed and hugged her friend. "Oh, Claire! I was just so worried about you. I thought feeding you was the best way to help. But seeing you laugh and be surrounded by friends is even better."

They both laughed until they cried, the tension of the past few weeks melting away. From that day on, Emma found other ways to support Claire—sometimes with a meal, but more often with a walk in the park or a chat over coffee.

Looking back, Claire and Emma often laugh about the *Great Food Flood*, as they call it. It became a reminder of how friends, despite the best intentions, can sometimes go a little overboard in their efforts to help. It also taught Claire the importance of honest communication, even when it's uncomfortable. Their friendship grew stronger through the experience, and the laughter they shared at that party became a cherished memory in Claire's journey of healing.

In the end, it wasn't just the food that helped Claire through her grief—it was the love, laughter, and support of her friends, each contributing in their own unique way. The story of the unwanted meals became a symbol of the unpredictable, sometimes comical, ways people show they care—and how, even in the darkest times, moments of joy and connection can shine through.

## Finding My Strength and Support

My family was my first source of support. My mother, equally heartbroken, became my grieving partner. We spent countless hours sharing stories about my father, laughing through tears as we remembered his quirks and his boundless love for us. My siblings, who had travelled from different parts of the country, brought with them a sense of unity and strength. We leaned on each other, finding comfort in our shared loss and the deep bonds that had always tied us together.

Friends, too, rallied around me. Richard, my childhood friend, was the first to arrive at my doorstep. He brought a bag of groceries and a hug that conveyed more than words ever could. Richard had known my father well and understood the depth of my pain. He stayed with me, helped with arrangements, and simply sat beside me in silence when words felt inadequate.

Colleagues sent flowers, cards, and heartfelt messages of condolence, reminding me that I was not alone in my grief. One colleague, James, who had lost his own father a few years prior, reached out to share his experience. His empathy and understanding provided a unique comfort, helping me navigate the complex emotions that come with losing a parent.

My father's friends also became an unexpected but significant source of support. Many had known him for decades, and their stories painted a picture of a man who was deeply loved and respected. They shared anecdotes that made me smile and cry, bringing my father's memory to life in new and beautiful ways. Their presence at the funeral was a testament to the impact he had on their lives, and their continued support helped me feel connected to him even after his passing.

One of the most surprising sources of comfort came from a grief support group I discovered through a local spiritual church. At first, I was hesitant—unsure if sharing my pain with strangers would truly help. But the group became a sanctuary. Each member had their own story of loss, and together we created a safe space to express our grief without fear of judgement. The connections I formed within that group became a vital part of my healing process.

Spiritual support also played a significant role. I found solace in attending church services and speaking with members of the congregation. Their gentle guidance and comforting words helped me navigate the spiritual dimensions of grief. They reminded me that my father's spirit lived on—not only in heaven, but in the love and memories we shared. Lighting a candle in his memory during each service became a peaceful ritual that brought me a sense of continuity and calm.

As time passed, the heavy fog of grief began to lift, replaced by a more manageable, though persistent, sadness. Slowly, I began to rediscover moments of joy—occasions when I could laugh and feel light-hearted again, free from the weight of guilt. This shift was only possible thanks to the incredible support network surrounding me.

Richard and I often reminisce about those early days, laughing at the absurdity of some situations and the overabundance of casseroles delivered by well-meaning neighbours. My family remained my anchor, our relationships strengthened by our shared experience of loss. The spiritual support group became a cornerstone of my weekly routine, offering a space to continue exploring my feelings and draw strength from others walking a similar path.

Looking back, I now see that the support I received formed a mosaic of love, empathy, and practical help. Every piece—be it family, friends, colleagues, or spiritual guidance—played a vital role in my journey through grief. They reminded me that while my father was gone, I was not alone. Their presence helped me find the strength to move forward, carrying my father's memory with me and honouring his legacy through the resilience they inspired in me.

Ultimately, it was the collective embrace of these incredible people that carried me through the darkest period of my life. They taught me that asking for and accepting help is not a sign of weakness, but a testament to the strength found in human connection. Through them, I discovered that although grief is a deeply personal journey, it need not be travelled alone.

# Chapter Six

## *Honouring and Remembering – Turning Grief Into Hope!*

The loss of a loved one is a profound experience that reshapes the landscape of our lives. In the aftermath of such a loss, finding ways to honour and remember the person who has passed becomes a vital part of the healing process. This chapter explores various meaningful ways to keep the memory of a loved one alive, ensuring that their legacy continues to inspire and comfort us.

### Creating Personal Memorials

One of the most intimate ways to honour a lost loved one is by creating personal memorials. These can take many forms, depending on what resonates most deeply with you. For some, it may be a small altar at home, adorned with photographs, candles, and cherished mementoes. This sacred space can serve as a daily reminder of your loved one—a place where you can feel close to them.

Others may find solace in planting a tree or creating a garden in their loved one's memory. Watching something grow and flourish can be a powerful symbol of life continuing and a reflection of your loved one's enduring presence in the world. Each time you tend the garden or rest beneath the tree, you nurture a living testament to their memory.

## Celebrating Anniversaries and Special Occasions

Anniversaries and special occasions—such as birthdays or holidays—can be particularly challenging after a loss. However, they also present unique opportunities to celebrate your loved one's life. You might choose to mark these dates with a family gathering, sharing stories, flipping through photo albums, or watching home videos. Such gatherings can become joyful celebrations of the time you shared, rather than solemn reminders of your grief.

On the anniversary of their passing, some find comfort in performing acts of kindness in their loved one's name. This might involve volunteering for a cause they cared about, making a charitable donation, or simply helping someone in need. These gestures not only honour your loved one's memory but also extend their legacy of compassion and generosity into the world.

## Keeping Traditions Alive

Maintaining family traditions is another meaningful way to remember a lost loved one. Whether it's a holiday ritual, a favourite recipe, or an annual trip, traditions carry the essence of your loved one and the memories you created together. By preserving these customs, you keep their presence woven into the fabric of your family's ongoing story.

For instance, if your loved one had a signature dish they always prepared for family gatherings, you could continue making that dish in their honour. Each time you cook it, you're not only preserving a part of their legacy but also creating new memories infused with their influence.

## Creating Art and Writing

Artistic expression can be a powerful channel for honouring a loved one. Many people find solace in creating artwork, writing poetry, or composing music inspired by their memories. These creative outlets allow you to process emotions and transform grief into something beautiful and lasting.

Writing can be particularly therapeutic. Keeping a journal where you pen letters to your loved one or record cherished memories can help you work through your grief and maintain a sense of connection. You might also consider writing a memoir or a collection of stories about your time together to share with family and future generations.

## Memorial Events and Gatherings

Organising a memorial event or gathering can be a profound way to celebrate a loved one's life. These events may range from formal ceremonies to informal get-togethers, where friends and family share stories, laughter, and remembrance. You might include speeches, musical tributes, or a slideshow of photos and videos.

A memorial gathering also provides an opportunity for collective healing. Sharing memories in a group setting can be immensely comforting and remind everyone of the impact your loved one had on many lives. Over time, these gatherings can evolve into cherished traditions, fostering a continued sense of community and connection.

## Living Their Values

One of the most enduring ways to honour a lost loved one is by living according to the values they held dear. Reflect on what mattered most to them—whether kindness, generosity, resilience, or love—and strive to embody those qualities in your own life. In doing so, you extend their legacy through your actions, influencing others just as they once influenced you.

If your loved one was passionate about a particular cause, consider getting involved. Whether it's environmental conservation, social justice, or community service, dedicating time and energy to something they cared about allows their spirit to live on through meaningful contributions.

## Creating Lasting Legacies

Establishing a lasting legacy is another significant way to remember a lost loved one. This might involve setting up scholarships, foundations, or charitable trusts in their name. Such initiatives provide continued support for causes they were passionate about and ensure their impact endures for generations.

For example, if your loved one was a teacher, a scholarship for aspiring educators would be a fitting tribute. If they were an artist, establishing an art award or grant for young talent could honour their creative spirit. These legacies not only preserve their memory but also reflect the values and passions that defined their life.

## Spiritual Practices and Rituals

For many, spiritual practices and rituals offer comfort and a sense of connection to their lost loved one. This may include prayer, meditation, or attending religious services. Engaging in these practices can provide peace and a feeling of closeness to the departed.

Creating personal rituals can also be deeply comforting. Lighting a candle at a set time, saying a daily prayer, or setting aside moments of silence for reflection can become grounding practices that reaffirm your ongoing bond with your loved one.

## Engaging with Nature

Nature has a remarkable ability to soothe and restore. Spending time outdoors whether hiking, gardening, or simply sitting in a park can help you feel connected to the broader cycles of life and death. Many find comfort in nature's continuity and its quiet, healing presence.

You might choose to dedicate a natural space to your loved one's memory by planting a tree, creating a memorial bench, or designing a small garden. These spaces become personal sanctuaries for reflection, remembrance, and peace.

## Embracing Community and Connection

Finally, one of the most powerful ways to honour a loved one is by nurturing the relationships and communities they were part of. Staying connected with their friends and family, sharing stories, and supporting one another keeps their memory alive.

It involves participating in community events or groups such as a book club, a volunteer organisation, or a local sports team. These groups provide continuity and connection. Through these shared experiences, you continue to feel passions and presence of your loved ones.

In conclusion, honouring and remembering a lost loved one is a deeply personal journey. There is no right or wrong way—only what feels meaningful and comforting to you. Whether through personal memorials, special celebrations, family traditions, artistic expression, community engagement, or spiritual practices, each act of remembrance becomes a thread in the enduring tapestry of their legacy. In keeping their memory alive, you allow their spirit to continue offering comfort, inspiration, and connection that transcends the boundaries of life and death.

## James' Story

The room was softly lit, the gentle hum of a fan providing a soothing background. As a psychic medium, I have witnessed countless stories of loss and healing, but each one continues to touch me deeply. This day was no exception.

A man named James had scheduled a session with me. When he arrived, his eyes were shadowed with sorrow, but there was a flicker of determination in them too.

"Hello, James," I greeted him warmly, gesturing for him to take a seat. I explained that I would connect with the spirit and share what I was being shown, and that he could simply confirm with a 'yes' or 'no'.

I closed my eyes and reached out to my spirit guide. Almost immediately it became apparent I was dealing with a very young soul that had passed recently. I looked into James' eyes and felt the pain that he had been going through. I had connected with Emily his 8-year-old daughter who had passed 12 months earlier with cancer. The journey I went on that day stays in my heart to this day. The courage that James and his family had shown and the heartache they had endured was unbearable for even me to contemplate.

It had become apparent there had been so much hope and happiness that a cure would have been found only to have all hope taken from them one cold November night. Emily told me the night she died, her father had walked into her bedroom, and hugged and cried into her dressing gown. Most people would find this heart wrenching but to James this was proof that Emily was there and only she could know about this.

Emily's spirit was radiating love and gratitude. "She wants you to remember the joy you shared and to know that she's always with you, cheering you on."

James's eyes widened, and he looked around the room as if he could see her too.

"She's here?" he whispered.

"Yes," I affirmed.

James' shoulders relaxed, and a peaceful expression spread across his face.

"Thank you," he said softly. "That means more to me than you can imagine."

As the reading went from sadness to almost happiness, Emily laughed at the fact her dad had removed a lock of her hair. This gave James a sense of knowing that Emily was with us that day. I assured her father that she was ok and that she wanted nothing more than for her family to move on.

After the reading, James took a deep breath, his hands trembling slightly as he settled into the chair across from me. "I lost my daughter, Emily, last year," he began, his voice thick with emotion. "She was only eight. She had a rare form of cancer, and despite our best efforts, we couldn't save her."

A wave of sympathy washed over me. The loss of a child is an unimaginable pain, and I could see the depth of James' grief etched into every line of his face. "I'm so sorry for your loss," I said softly. "Tell me about Emily."

James' eyes softened as he spoke of his daughter. "She was the brightest light in our lives. Always smiling, always thinking of others—even when she was in pain. Emily had this incredible way of making everyone around her feel special."

He paused, a small smile playing on his lips as he recalled her.

"Before she passed, she told me she wanted to help other children who were sick. She said she didn't want anyone else to feel alone."

Tears welled up in James' eyes, and he took a moment to compose himself.

"That's why I'm here," he continued. "After Emily died, I didn't know how to go on. I felt lost, angry, and empty. But then I remembered her wish. I decided to start a charity in her name, to support families and children going through similar battles."

Over the next few months, James threw himself into building Emily's charity. He named it *Emily's Light*, and its mission was clear: to provide emotional and financial support to families with terminally ill children. He organised fundraisers, charity runs, and community events—all aimed at raising awareness and funds for the cause.

One of the first major events was a charity gala. James poured his heart into planning it, ensuring every detail was perfect. On the night of the gala, the room was filled with people whose lives had been touched by Emily's story. There were families who had received support from the charity, doctors and nurses who had treated Emily, and friends and relatives who wanted to honour her memory.

As James took the stage to speak, he felt a surge of emotion. He began by sharing Emily's story—her courage and her wish to help others.

*"Emily's Light is not just a charity,"* he said, his voice steady and strong. *"It's a testament to the power of love*

*and the impact one small, beautiful life can have on the world."*

The audience was moved to tears, and many pledged their support. By the end of the night, the charity had raised an incredible sum of money, far exceeding James's expectations.

In the months and years that followed, *Emily's Light* grew and flourished. It funded medical treatments, provided counselling services, and created a supportive community for families facing the unthinkable. Each success was a tribute to Emily's spirit and her father's unwavering dedication.

James continued to visit me for readings, finding comfort in knowing that Emily was always close by. During one session, she shared a message that stayed with him forever.

*"Daddy,"* she said through me, *"you turned my dream into real life. Thank you for keeping my light alive. I'm always with you, and I love you."*

Those words became James' guiding star. They reminded him that, despite the pain of loss, there was still beauty and purpose to be found. *Emily's Light* was not just a charity; it was a beacon of hope—a testament to the enduring power of love—and a way for a father's devotion to transform grief into a legacy of compassion and support.

* * *

When my father passed away, the world seemed to lose its colour. The vibrant hues of everyday life dimmed, and a heavy weight of sorrow settled in my heart. The days blurred together as I struggled to comprehend a future without him. My father had been my anchor—a constant source of wisdom, love, and support. His absence left a void that seemed impossible to fill. Yet, amid the grief, I knew I had to find a way to honour his memory and keep his spirit alive.

One of the first decisions I made was to create a personal memorial in my home. I cleared a small corner in my bedroom and set up a space with some of my father's belongings—a lock of his hair, a small ring, and photographs from family gatherings. I placed a candle there and lit it each evening as a ritual of remembrance. This small altar became a sanctuary where I could feel his presence and reflect on the moments we had shared.

Music had always been a significant part of my father's life. His love for artists like Johnny Mathis was something that bonded us, filling our home with melodies that echoed his spirit and zest for life. I knew that one of the most profound ways to remember and honour him was through the music that had brought him so much joy.

Listening to my father's favourite music became a daily ritual. I would play Johnny Mathis records, letting the smooth, soulful notes wash over me as I drove or relaxed after work. Songs like *"Chances Are"* and *"Misty"* transported me back to the days when my father would sing along, his eyes closed, completely immersed in the moment. It was as if, through the music, I could still hear his voice and feel his presence beside me. These moments offered solace—a way to reconnect with my father and keep his memory alive.

As a special tribute, my family and I decided to attend a Johnny Mathis concert. It seemed fitting to celebrate my father's life through a live performance of the music he had cherished. We managed to secure tickets for a show in the city, and the anticipation leading up to the event was palpable. My siblings, mother, and I shared stories and memories of my father, each anecdote interwoven with the melodies he had loved. The concert became a beacon of connection and remembrance—a way to honour my father as a family.

The night of the concert was magical. As we took our seats and the lights dimmed, a wave of emotion swept over me. Johnny Mathis took the stage, and the first notes of his music filled the air. I looked around at my family—united in this tribute—and felt a sense of peace and closeness. When Johnny sang *"Wonderful! Wonderful!"* I closed my eyes and could almost see my father swaying to the music, a smile on his face. The concert was more than a performance—it was a living memory, a way to feel my father's presence and celebrate his love for music.

One of his favourite places to dine was a quaint Italian bistro known for its incredible steaks and warm atmosphere. The first time we visited after his passing was bittersweet. Walking in, I half-expected to see him at our usual table, perusing the menu with his characteristic enthusiasm. We ordered his favourite dishes—fillet steak with chips, garlic bread, and tiramisu—and toasted to his memory. Sharing a meal at his favourite restaurant felt like a fitting tribute, a way to honour his culinary passion and keep our family traditions alive.

Another favourite was a local club where my father loved to spend Saturday nights. The staff knew him by name, and the regulars all held fond memories of him. When we visited, we were greeted with warm smiles and heartfelt condolences. Staff members shared their stories of my father, and we reminisced about the many evenings spent there—savouring not just the food and entertainment, but also the simple, precious moments of togetherness.

Through these visits, we found a unique way to celebrate my father's life. Each meal—each bite—was a reminder of the joy he found in good food and good company. It became a tradition for us to gather at his favourite spots on special occasions—his birthday, Father's Day, and the anniversary of his passing. These meals were not only about remembering the past but also about creating new memories in his honour, ensuring that his love for dining out lived on through us.

Music and food became the cornerstones of our remembrance. They were more than mere hobbies or preferences; they were expressions of my father's personality and passions. By immersing ourselves in the melodies he adored and the flavours he relished, we kept his spirit vibrant and present in our lives.

The concert and the meals at his favourite restaurants taught us that remembrance can be both a joyous celebration and a heartfelt tribute. Through these acts, we found a way to transform our grief into moments of connection, honouring my father's legacy in ways that brought comfort and unity. His love for music and food became a guiding light, reminding us that although he was no longer physically with us, his spirit continued to inspire and bring us together.

Remembering my father's passing became an ongoing journey of honouring his life and legacy. Through personal memorials, shared stories, and preserved traditions, we as a family discovered ways to keep his spirit alive. These acts of remembrance transformed my grief into a celebration of his life, ensuring that his memory continued to inspire and comfort me. In these moments of reflection and tribute, I came to understand that although he was no longer physically present, his love and influence would always be a part of me, guiding me forward with strength and grace.

# Chapter Seven
## *Navigating Special Days*

The loss of a loved one casts a long shadow over life's most celebrated moments. Special days and holidays, once anticipated with joy, can become painful reminders of absence and grief. Navigating these occasions without the person who was once so integral to them is a profound challenge. It requires a delicate balance of honouring their memory while also discovering new ways to experience joy and connection.

In the months leading up to the first anniversary, birthday, or special occasion after the loss, the anticipation of familiar celebrations can feel overwhelming. Every decoration and festive song serves as a stark reminder of the missing presence. For many, the approach of these days is accompanied by a mix of dread and sorrow. The preparations, once a source of excitement, now feel burdensome. Tasks such as decorating the tree, baking traditional treats, or buying gifts may amplify the void left by the loved one's absence.

Families often find solace in creating new traditions that honour their loved one's memory. One family member who visited me told me they decided to gather on Christmas Eve to share stories about their father, who had recently passed away. They recounted favourite memories and the qualities that made him special. This storytelling ritual became a way of keeping his spirit alive. Sitting around the fire, they laughed and cried together, finding comfort in their shared experiences. These moments of remembrance offered a sense of continuity, allowing them to celebrate his life even while mourning his loss.

Acts of kindness and charity can also offer meaningful ways to navigate the holidays. Many people find that giving back to the community helps channel their grief into something positive. Volunteering at a local shelter or participating in charity drives can be a way to honour a loved one's values and spirit. One family chose to serve meals at a homeless shelter on Christmas Day, inspired by their mother's lifelong commitment to helping others. This act of service became a new tradition, bringing them closer together and helping them feel her guiding influence.

Special days such as birthdays and anniversaries can be particularly difficult. These milestones are deeply personal, and the absence of the loved one is often keenly felt. For one woman, her mother's birthday was a time of profound sorrow. To honour her memory, she decided to spend the day doing the things her mother loved: cooking her favourite meal, playing her favourite songs, and visiting her favourite park. These activities brought a bittersweet comfort, allowing her to feel connected to her mother in a tangible way. It wasn't the same, but it was a heartfelt way to keep her memory alive.

Another family found comfort in maintaining some of their old traditions while introducing new ones. They continued to hold their annual holiday dinner, setting a place at the table for their loved one. This empty chair served as a silent tribute—a way to acknowledge their absence while celebrating their life. They also created a new tradition: each year, they would write messages to their loved one on paper lanterns and release them into the sky. Watching the lanterns drift upwards, they felt a sense of peace and connection, as though their words might somehow reach the person they missed.

Some find comfort in the language of the natural world—a candle's glow mirroring the warmth of memory, the rustle of leaves carrying whispered echoes, the stillness of a star-filled night holding space for unspoken love. Others would prefer to remember in more religious or spiritual ways. In these quiet moments, the presence of the one who has gone feels near, woven gently into the world around us.

One man found comfort in visiting his church every Sunday, where he would light a candle in memory of his wife. This simple act became a weekly ritual—a way to feel close to her and draw strength from his faith. The church community offered support and understanding, becoming an extended family that shared in his grief and remembrance.

The emotional landscape of special days and holidays is often complex. There are moments of deep sorrow, but also flashes of joy and laughter. It's important to honour these emotions, allowing oneself to grieve while remaining open to lightness and warmth. Some people find it helpful to speak openly about their loved one, sharing memories and stories with family and friends.

Others may prefer quiet reflection, drawing peace from solitude or nature.

Grief can be unpredictable, and it is essential to be gentle with oneself. There will be days when the sorrow feels overwhelming, and that is perfectly natural. It is also natural to experience joy, to laugh, and to find moments of happiness amidst the pain. These emotions are not mutually exclusive—they coexist as part of the human experience.

Support from others is vital. Leaning on friends and family, joining a support group, seeking spiritual guidance, or speaking to a therapist can provide much-needed comfort and understanding. One woman joined a bereavement group after the death of her mother and found healing in the shared stories and empathy of those who had experienced similar loss. These connections offered her a sense of community and helped her through the most difficult days.

Ultimately, navigating special days and holidays after losing a loved one is a deeply personal journey. There is no right or wrong way to grieve or to honour their memory. What matters most is finding a path that feels authentic and meaningful—one that allows for both the pain of loss and the joy of remembrance. Whether through new traditions, charitable acts, spiritual practices, or quiet reflection, it is possible to approach these days with grace and resilience. In doing so, the memory of our loved one becomes a guiding light, illuminating the path forward and keeping their spirit alive in the hearts of those who remember them.

## Ways to Help Manage These Difficult Times:

- **Create New Traditions:** *Establish activities that honour your loved one's memory, such as cooking their favourite meal or visiting a special place they cherished.*
- **Storytelling and Sharing Memories:** *Spend time with family and friends recounting stories and fond memories. This can provide comfort and keep their spirit alive.*
- **Volunteer or Give Back:** *Engage in acts of kindness. Volunteering in your loved one's name can be a powerful way to honour their values and legacy.*
- **Visit Their Favourite Places:** *Spending time in locations that held meaning for your loved one can offer a sense of closeness and reflection.*
- **Set Aside Quiet Time:** *Make space for personal reflection, prayer, or meditation. These moments can foster emotional clarity and connection.*

- **Light a Candle or Create a Memorial:** *A small, meaningful tribute—such as lighting a candle or setting up a memorial at home—can provide comfort and a sense of presence.*
- **Continue Old Traditions:** *Maintaining traditions they enjoyed can bring continuity and connection during difficult times.*
- • **Put Your Feelings Into Words** – Like sketching the outlines of a landscape, capture your memories and emotions on paper. Letting them take shape can bring gentle clarity.
- • **Lean On Your Connections** – Just as trees support one another in a forest, reach out to those who can offer quiet understanding and steady presence. Shared care can lighten even the heaviest moments.
- • **Flow with Your Emotions** – Emotions, like the tides or the changing seasons, come and go. Allow each one to move through you in its own time, allowing the natural rhythm of grief.
- **Plan Ahead:** *If certain dates are especially difficult, schedule activities that bring meaning or distraction to help you cope.*
- **Celebrate Their Life:** *On significant anniversaries, consider a family gathering, a memorial event, or a special outing in their honour.*
- • **Nourish Your Own Roots** – Just as plants need sunlight, water, and care, give yourself what you need to stay grounded. Small acts of rest and self-kindness can help you weather the storm of grief.
- • **Open Your Heart Like A Window** – Let trusted voices and gentle presence in, allowing warmth and understanding to flow in.

Connection can act as a quiet anchor when emotions run deep.

These strategies can help you navigate the emotional complexities of special days and holidays, enabling you to honour your loved one's memory while also caring for yourself.

## Anna's Story:

It was just a month before their wedding day when Anna received the devastating news. Her fiancé, Jake—the love of her life and her best friend—had been in a car accident. He hadn't survived. In an instant, all the dreams they had built together were shattered. Her wedding dress hung in the wardrobe like a ghost, a cruel reminder of what was meant to be the happiest day of her life.

Anna was plunged into a deep grief that seemed inescapable. Their small apartment, once alive with wedding preparations, now felt like a mausoleum. Everywhere she turned, there were reminders of Jake—his favourite coffee mug, his books, his clothes. Friends and family surrounded her with love and support, but nothing could fill the void left by his absence.

As the weeks turned into months, Anna struggled to find a way to move forward. Her days were filled with an unbearable silence. One day, while sorting through Jake's belongings, she found a letter tucked away in his drawer. It was addressed to her, meant to be read on the morning of their wedding. With trembling hands, she opened it.

In the letter, Jake spoke of his love for her, his excitement for their future, and his belief that their love could withstand anything life might throw at them. He ended with a line that struck Anna deeply: *"Even if I'm not with you, I'll always be by your side. Love, Jake."*

Inspired by his words, Anna resolved to find a way to honour Jake's memory—to keep him close, even though he was gone. She remembered how much he had loved stargazing. It had been one of their favourite activities: lying on a blanket under the night sky, pointing out constellations, and dreaming about their future.

Anna decided to buy a telescope and learn more about the stars. She joined an astronomy club, and soon, gazing at the night sky became a way for her to feel connected to Jake. On what would have been their wedding night, she returned to their favourite stargazing spot. She brought a blanket, a bottle of wine, and the telescope. As she lay there, looking up at the vast expanse of the universe, she felt Jake's presence beside her, as though he were watching the stars with her.

This became her new ritual. Whenever she missed Jake, she would return to their special spot and stargaze. Each time she discovered a new constellation or saw a shooting star, she took it as a message from him. The stars, in their infinite beauty, became symbols of their eternal love.

One night, Anna saw a bright star and felt a profound sense of peace wash over her. She decided to name it after Jake. She contacted an organisation that allowed people to name stars, and soon, a star in the night sky officially bore his name. It comforted her to know that his memory was now etched in the cosmos.

Anna also began volunteering at a local observatory, sharing her passion for the stars with others. She found joy in teaching children about constellations and watching their faces light up with wonder. It was a way to honour Jake's love for stargazing and to keep his spirit alive. Through these activities, Anna found a renewed sense of purpose, channelling her grief into something meaningful.

On the anniversary of what would have been their wedding day, Anna organised a special stargazing event for her friends and family. They gathered at the observatory, where she delivered a heartfelt speech about Jake, their love, and how the stars had become her solace. Together, they watched the night sky, feeling Jake's presence in the twinkling lights above.

This annual event became a cherished tradition—a way for everyone who loved Jake to come together and celebrate his life. They would share stories, laugh, cry, and gaze at the star that bore his name. It was a night of remembrance and healing, a testament to the idea that love never truly dies.

Anna's journey through grief was far from easy, but in finding a way to honour Jake's memory, she discovered a path to healing. The stars, with their eternal light, became symbols of the love they had shared. Through stargazing, she found a way to keep him close, to celebrate his life, and to navigate her own future.

Anna knew that Jake would always be a part of her, guiding her from the heavens. Each time she looked up at the night sky, she felt his love shining down on her—a love that would never fade, no matter how many miles of space lay between them.

## Reflections on Remembrance:

In the aftermath of losing a loved one, there is no one-size-fits-all approach to remembrance. Each person's way of honouring a loved one is as unique as the relationship they shared. The grieving process is deeply personal, and so too is the journey of remembrance. It's important to recognise that there are countless ways to commemorate those we've lost, and what matters most is that the remembrance feels meaningful to those left behind.

The diversity of remembrance practices reflects the unique bonds formed during a loved one's life. For some, traditional rituals offer comfort—such as holding a memorial service or creating a shrine filled with photographs, mementoes, and cherished belongings. These practices provide structure, allowing people to express grief and celebrate a life well lived. Memorial services might include eulogies, personal stories, and music that held significance for the deceased. For many, such gatherings bring comfort and a sense of closure.

Others find solace in creating something new in honour of their loved one. Someone might plant a garden dedicated to a nature-loving relative, while another may establish a scholarship or charity fund in their name, channelling grief into a cause close to their heart. These legacy projects not only honour the memory of the departed but also allow their spirit to live on through meaningful contributions.

Artistic expression is another powerful avenue for remembrance. Some may paint, write poetry, or compose music that reflects their emotions and memories. Others may pen novels inspired by the life and personality of their loved one. Such creative endeavours offer a deeply personal outlet for grief, transforming pain into something beautiful and enduring.

For those who shared meaningful experiences with the deceased, continuing these activities can be a powerful way to remember them. If a loved one enjoyed hiking, surviving family members might take a commemorative hike and place a memorial plaque along a favourite trail.

If they loved cooking, recreating their favourite dishes and sharing them with others can help keep their memory alive in daily life.

Spiritual practices also play a vital role in remembrance.

Some seek refuge in whispered prayers or the soft rhythm of meditation, letting the silence wrap around them like a warm cloak. Others kindle flames in the darkness, lay offerings with tender hands, or move through ancient rituals that speak the language of the soul. In these moments, peace drifts in like a quiet tide, and the space between the living and the departed feels as thin as breath.

The manner in which people choose to remember their loved ones is not governed by external expectations. It is shaped by the relationship they had and what feels right for them. Some find comfort in solitude, while others draw strength from community. Some prefer quiet reflection, while others are uplifted by sharing stories and experiences.

It's important to honour and respect the diversity of remembrance practices. What feels meaningful to one person may not resonate with another—and that's okay.

This variety reflects the richness of human relationships and the individuality of grief. What matters most is that remembrance feels genuine and healing.

In sharing stories of how people remember those they've lost, we see that there is no right or wrong way to honour a life. Whether through grand gestures or small daily rituals, each act of remembrance is a reflection of love and connection. The essence of remembrance lies not in its form, but in the intention and heart behind it.

Ultimately, the most important aspect of remembrance is that it brings comfort and fosters connection. It enables the grieving to carry their loved one's legacy forward in a way that feels authentic. Whether through traditional ceremonies, creative projects, spiritual observances, or personal habits, the ways we remember are as varied as the lives we seek to honour.

As we navigate grief, we come to understand that remembering is a journey—one of discovering what brings us peace and keeps our loved ones alive in our hearts. Each act of remembrance becomes a tribute: a unique expression of love, memory, and enduring connection. Embracing this diversity allows us to better understand and appreciate how we continue to carry those we've lost with us, even as we move forward with our lives.

# Chapter Eight

*Moving Forward*

## Moving Forward After the Loss of a Loved One

It is a profoundly difficult journey that tests the very fabric of our emotional and psychological resilience. The void left by their absence can feel all-encompassing, making it seem impossible to imagine a future without them. However, while the pain may never completely disappear, it is possible to find a way to live with it and eventually experience joy and fulfilment once more.

Grief is an intensely personal experience, manifesting differently for everyone. Some may find themselves engulfed in waves of sadness, while others might experience anger, confusion, or even numbness. It's crucial to understand that all these emotions are valid and part of the natural grieving process. Recognising and accepting these feelings is the first step towards healing. This acknowledgement allows one to process the loss rather than suppress it—something that can otherwise lead to more significant emotional complications over time.

In the immediate aftermath of a loss, the world often feels like it's in a state of suspended animation. Everyday routines become disorienting, and even the simplest tasks can seem insurmountable. Establishing a new routine can provide a sense of normalcy and stability during this turbulent period. Even small actions, such as having regular mealtimes or going for daily walks, can serve as anchors and help reintroduce a sense of order into your life.

Seeking support is another vital part of moving forward. Grief can be isolating, but it's important to remember that you don't have to navigate this journey alone. Friends and family can offer comfort and companionship—a listening ear and a shoulder to cry on.

Expert Advice, such as grief counselling or therapy, can also be invaluable. Therapists can offer coping strategies, help process complex emotions, and provide a safe space to express feelings without judgement.

Expressing emotions through creative outlets can also be incredibly therapeutic. Writing, whether in a journal or as letters to the deceased, allows for the expression of thoughts and feelings that may be too painful to share aloud. Art, music, and other forms of creative expression can act as conduits for grief, offering a way to release emotions and create something meaningful from the pain.

Physical health often takes a backseat during grieving, yet maintaining it is essential. Grief can sap energy and motivation, making self-care all the more important. Regular exercise—even gentle activities such as yoga or walking—can improve mood and overall wellbeing. A balanced diet and adequate sleep are equally vital, as they support both physical and mental health during this challenging time.

As you navigate through grief, there may come a point when you begin to search for meaning in the loss. This search is a natural part of the healing process. It involves reflecting on the impact of your loved one's life and their enduring influence. Such reflection can lead to personal growth and a re-evaluation of your values and priorities. Finding meaning doesn't diminish the pain, but it can provide a sense of purpose and direction.

Creating a legacy or tribute for the deceased can be a powerful way to honour their memory. This might involve charitable work, establishing a scholarship, or simply continuing traditions that were important to them.

These actions not only keep their memory alive but also transform the loss into something positive and life-affirming.

Rebuilding life after such a profound loss involves redefining your identity and discovering new sources of joy and purpose. Setting small, achievable goals can support this process. These goals offer direction and a sense of accomplishment, fostering a renewed sense of motivation. Exploring new interests and hobbies can also be deeply fulfilling, opening up new avenues for joy and engagement.

Strengthening existing relationships and forging new ones is another important step. Open communication with loved ones can deepen connections and provide mutual support. It may also be helpful to seek out others who have experienced similar losses, as they can offer unique understanding and empathy.

Ultimately, moving forward after the loss of a loved one is about acceptance and integration. Acceptance doesn't mean forgetting or 'moving on' from the person you've lost; rather, it means finding a way to live with the absence. It involves acknowledging the permanent impact of the loss while still looking ahead. This acceptance allows the loss to become part of your ongoing story, rather than an insurmountable barrier.

Embracing change is an integral part of this journey. Life after loss is inherently different, and resisting that change can hinder healing. Embracing the new reality—with all its challenges and opportunities—allows for growth and new beginnings. Practising gratitude can also shift your focus from what has been lost to what remains. Daily gratitude, even for small things, can improve mental wellbeing and foster a more positive outlook on life.

Moving forward after the loss of a loved one is a complex, deeply personal journey. It requires time, patience, and immense self-compassion. While the pain may never fully disappear, it is possible to live a meaningful and fulfilling life once again. By honouring the past while embracing the future, you can find a way to move forward—carrying the memory of your loved one with you in a way that enriches your life and brings you peace.

## Clara's Story

It was a blustery autumn afternoon when the doorbell rang. I opened the door to find a woman standing there, her demeanour a mixture of desperation and hope.

"Hello," she began, her voice quivering slightly. "My name is Clara. Clara Wilson. I heard about you from a friend. They said you might be able to help me find some peace."

I invited her in, noting the deep lines etched into her face, signs of prolonged sorrow. Clara's eyes, though kind, seemed haunted by a burden she had carried for far too long. She sat down on the sofa, glancing around as if searching for reassurance.

"Would you like some tea?" I offered, trying to ease the initial awkwardness. She nodded appreciatively.

I decided it was time to use my gift. As a psychic medium, I had helped many people connect with their departed loved ones. I explained the process to Clara, emphasising that the goal was to find peace—not to cling to false hope.

We prepared a quiet space in my living room, dimming the lights and lighting a few candles to create a serene atmosphere. Clara sat nervously, clutching her teacup with trembling hands.

"Close your eyes and take a few deep breaths," I instructed gently. "Think about your loved one—about the love you shared and the good times. Invite them to join us."

As Clara began to relax, I closed my eyes and focused, reaching out to my spirit guide to connect with the other side. After a few moments, I felt a presence—warm and familiar. Along with that I felt pain in my chest. I opened my eyes to find Clara looking at me expectantly.

"Thomas is here," I said softly. "He wants you to know that he loves you and that he's been watching over you." As I said this, my hand involuntarily moved to my chest where I was feeling unease and Clara nodded to me knowingly! Sometimes, I experience the pain that the spirit has been through that visits me during these meetings. This confirms their presence to their family members.

Clara's eyes widened, tears streaming down her cheeks. "Is he... is he okay?"

"He's more than okay," I assured her. "He's at peace. But he's concerned about you. He wants you to find happiness again—to live your life fully."

Thomas' presence grew stronger as I conveyed his messages to Clara. He spoke of their life together, sharing memories only the two of them would know. He reminded her of their dreams, their love, and his wish for her to find joy again.

"He says you need to let go of the guilt," I told her gently. "He knows you feel like you're betraying him by moving on, but he wants you to be happy. He wants you to live your life for both of you."

Clara sobbed quietly, the weight of her grief beginning to lift. "I've missed him so much. I didn't know how to move on without him."

"He's never truly gone," I reassured her. "His love is still with you. He will always be a part of you. But it's time to embrace the future—to find new joys and experiences. That's what he wants for you."

I shared more details with Clara that I received from Thomas and the life they had shared. I could see Clara becoming more at ease, visibly comforted by the information that resonated so deeply with her. As we spoke about the loving husband Thomas had been, a sense of calm seemed to settle over her.

Once I had finished conveying his messages, her words came spilling out like a long-held flood. “My husband, Thomas, passed away seven years ago. It was sudden—a heart attack. One moment he was there, and the next, he was gone. I haven’t been able to move on since. It’s like I’m trapped in that moment.”

She paused, tears welling up in her eyes. “Everyone tells me I should be over it by now, that I need to move forward. But I don’t know how. I feel him everywhere—in our house, in our favourite places, even in my dreams.”

I sat opposite her, listening intently. “Grief is a journey, Clara. It’s different for everyone, and there is no set timeline for healing.”

She sighed deeply, as if releasing some of the weight she carried.
“I came here because I heard you help people connect with their loved ones who have passed. I didn't know

what to expect, but I had to try something. I can't live like this anymore."

She was immensely grateful to have received messages from her beloved husband, and I felt truly honoured to have helped her ease some of her sorrow that day.

Clara's journey through grief had been a solitary one. After Thomas' death, she withdrew into the home they had lovingly built together. She left her job, unable to endure the pitying glances of colleagues, and over time, friends and family drifted away, unable to breach the walls of her sorrow.

For seven years, Clara lived in the past. Every corner of her house held a memory of Thomas: the kitchen table where they shared morning coffee, the garden they had tended together, the living room where they spent countless evenings talking about their dreams. Each memory, though precious, had become a shackle, preventing her from stepping into the future.

"I haven't touched his things," Clara admitted. "His clothes are still in the wardrobes, his books on the shelf. I can't bear to pack them away. It feels like erasing him."

I nodded, recognising the delicate balance between holding on and letting go.

"Perhaps it's not about erasing him, but about carrying his memory with you in a healthier way."

Clara looked at me, her eyes reflecting both hope and scepticism.
"How do I do that?"

"Tell me about Thomas," I suggested. "What was he like?"

Her expression softened as she began to speak about her late husband.

"He was kind, always helping others. He loved to laugh and made everyone around him feel special. He was my best friend."

Over the following weeks, Clara continued to visit. Each session brought more messages from Thomas—more reassurance that he was at peace and wished the same for her. Clara began to heal, gradually but surely. She started to re-engage with life: joining a local book club, volunteering at a community centre, and even tending the garden they once cherished together.

One day, Clara brought me a small potted plant. “It’s for you,” she said with a smile. “Thomas always believed in giving back, and I want to do the same. You’ve helped me more than you know.”

As the seasons changed, so did Clara. She was no longer the grief-stricken woman who had first knocked on my door. She had begun to find peace—not by forgetting Thomas, but by weaving his memory into a new chapter of her life.

On the anniversary of Thomas’ passing, Clara hosted a small gathering in her garden. Friends and family who had gradually drifted away returned, and for the first time, Clara spoke openly about her journey through grief.

“I’ve learnt that moving on doesn’t mean forgetting,” she said, her voice steady. “It means finding a way to live with the loss—to honour the memories while embracing the future.”

The garden, once a place of sorrow, now echoed with laughter and life. Clara had found her way forward, carrying Thomas’ memory not as a burden, but as a part of who she was.

As I left that evening, I felt a profound sense of fulfilment. Clara's journey was a testament to her strength, and a reminder that even in the darkest times, there is always a way to find light, to rediscover hope, and to move forward. Through my gift, I had helped her reconnect with her past and embrace her future—and in doing so, I had witnessed the remarkable resilience of the human spirit.

## Moving Forward After Loss: Unconventional Paths to Healing

Moving forward after losing a loved one can be incredibly challenging, and sometimes conventional advice doesn't resonate. Here are some lesser-known yet powerful steps that may help you navigate grief and discover your own path to healing:

- **Write Letters to Your Loved One**
  *Instead of simply journalling, try writing letters to your loved one. Share your thoughts, your daily experiences, and how much you miss them. This can foster a sense of continued connection.*
- **Create a Memory Box**
  *Collect cherished items—photos, letters, mementoes—and place them in a special box. Revisit it when you need comfort. It's a tangible way to honour their memory and keep their presence close.*

- **Establish a Daily Ritual**
  *Create a meaningful daily practice, such as lighting a candle, saying a prayer, or spending a few quiet moments in reflection. Rituals can offer solace and a sense of continuity.*
- **Engage in Creative Expression**
  *Use art to channel your emotions—paint, sculpt, write poetry, compose music. Creative outlets can give voice to feelings that words often cannot express.*
- **Practise Mindful Grieving**
  *Integrate mindfulness into your grief. Sit with your emotions each day, accepting them without judgement. This approach encourages emotional clarity and self-compassion.*
- **Volunteer or Support Others**
  *Helping others can foster connection and purpose. Consider volunteering at a charity, community group, or hospice. Acts of service can be both grounding and healing.*
- **Take Grief on a Journey**
  *Travel to a place that held meaning for your loved one—or somewhere they dreamt of visiting. Create new memories in their honour and allow travel to shift your perspective.*
- **Try a Physical Challenge**
  *Physical activity can be an emotional release. Train for a marathon, go hiking, or take up a new sport. Movement helps process grief and promotes mental well-being.*
- **Create a Tribute Project**
  *Honour your loved one through a meaningful project—a community garden, scholarship,*

*memorial website, or a collection of memories from family and friends. Let their legacy inspire others.*

- **Adopt a Pet**
  *If you're an animal lover, consider adopting a pet. Their companionship and unconditional love can be a source of comfort, and their care offers routine and responsibility.*
- **Attend a Grief Retreat or Workshop**
  *Structured healing environments—like grief retreats or workshops—can be immensely helpful. They often include nature therapy, group support, and expert guidance.*
- **Use Aromatherapy**
  *Scent can influence mood. Essential oils like lavender, chamomile, and frankincense have calming properties that may ease anxiety and support relaxation.*
- **Create a Healing Soundtrack**
  *Curate a playlist of songs that evoke memories or support emotional release. Music is a powerful, cathartic way to connect with and process your grief.*
- **Start a Gratitude Practice**
  *Though it may feel counterintuitive, gratitude can shift your focus toward what still brings you joy. Each day, write down a few things you're grateful for to gradually foster a more hopeful mindset.*
- **Embrace Nature Therapy**
  *Time in nature can be deeply restorative. Walk through the woods, visit a beach, or simply sit beneath a tree. The natural world offers quiet strength and grounding presence.*

- **Explore Alternative Healing Practices**
  *Consider Reiki, acupuncture, or energy healing. These approaches may support emotional balance and provide comfort alongside traditional therapies.*
- **Share Your Story**
  *Writing a book or blog about your grief journey can be both therapeutic and inspiring to others. It gives voice to your pain and purpose to your experience.*
- **Create a Vision Board**
  *Imagine your future and craft a visual board of your goals, dreams, and affirmations. Let it reflect the life you wish to build as you move forward.*

These unconventional paths offer a variety of ways to navigate grief. Choose the ones that resonate most with you. Above all, be patient and gentle with yourself—healing is not linear, and your journey will unfold at its own pace.

## Rachel – A Mother's Grief

Rachel had always been a strong woman. She had weathered life's storms with resilience and grace, raising her two children, Holly and James, with all the love and care she could give. She had been a single mother for most of their lives, but despite the challenges, she had created a warm and loving home. Holly, her eldest, was the light of her life—a bright, creative soul who had always been deeply sensitive to the world around her. But that sensitivity came with its own burdens—burdens that Rachel hadn't fully understood until it was too late.

Holly had struggled with depression for years, although she had hidden much of her pain behind a brave smile and a talent for helping others. Rachel knew her daughter had difficult days, but she never imagined the depth of Holly's despair. She never expected that one morning, she would find her baby girl gone—having taken her own life in the quiet of the night.

Rachel's world shattered. The pain of losing Holly was unlike anything she had ever experienced—a deep, gnawing agony that threatened to consume her. The grief was overwhelming, and Rachel found herself drowning in it, unable to see a way forward. Her once vibrant home now felt like a cold, empty shell, echoing with the silence left by her daughter's absence.

Days blurred into nights as Rachel drifted through them in a fog of sorrow. She couldn't eat, couldn't sleep, couldn't function. The only thing she could think about was Holly—her smile, her laugh, the way she used to curl up beside her on the couch and talk about her dreams. And now, all those dreams were gone, snuffed out by a darkness Rachel hadn't seen coming.

The guilt was unbearable. Rachel replayed every conversation, every moment she might have missed, searching for signs—anything she could have done differently. *If only* she had known. *If only* she had been there more, loved her more—maybe, just maybe, Holly would still be here. The weight of those thoughts crushed her, leaving her breathless and hopeless.

As the days turned into weeks, Rachel's grief took a darker turn. The idea of living without Holly became more than she could bear. She didn't want to go on, didn't want to face a future without her daughter. The thought of joining Holly—of ending her own pain and being with her baby girl again—began to take root in her mind. It was a terrifying thought, but at the same time, it felt like the only escape.

One evening, as Rachel sat alone in Holly's room, clutching her daughter's favourite stuffed animal, she reached out to the only person she thought might understand—her best friend, Sarah. Between sobs, she confessed the thoughts that had been haunting her: the unbearable longing to be with Holly, the despair that had overtaken her life.

Sarah listened quietly, her heart breaking for her friend. When Rachel finally fell silent, Sarah spoke gently, choosing her words with care.

"Rach, I know you're hurting more than I could ever truly understand. But I need you to hear me. There's someone I'd like you to talk to—someone who might be able to help, to offer you a sense of comfort. His name is John Hughes, and he's a psychic medium. I know it sounds strange, but I think you should go and see him. Maybe he can help you connect with Holly in some way—help you find a little peace."

Rachel was sceptical. She had never believed in psychics or mediums, and she wasn't sure anyone could help her now. But Sarah's words planted a small seed of hope, and in her desperation, Rachel agreed to make an appointment. She had nothing left to lose.

A few days later, Rachel found herself sitting with me. I didn't rush her or press her to talk. Instead, I asked her to close her eyes, breathe deeply, and open herself to whatever might come through.

"Rachel, I'm sensing a young woman here. She's full of love and light, but she's also deeply sorry for the pain she's caused you. She wants you to know that she's at peace now—that the darkness she felt has lifted. She's free, but she hasn't left you. She's been with you every day, watching over you, trying to comfort you." Rachel's eyes filled with tears.

"She's saying that she didn't want to leave you," I continued. "She says she was overwhelmed by her pain, but she never meant to hurt you. She's asking you to forgive her and to know that her love for you remains unchanged. And there's something else... She wants you to live, Rachel. She wants you to find joy again, even though it feels impossible right now. She's telling me that it's not your time—that you still have more to do here. She'll be waiting for you, but she wants you to stay, to live—for both of you."

Rachel broke down, tears flowing freely as she listened to the words that could only have come from her beloved Holly. The phrases were so familiar, the sentiments so deeply entwined with their relationship, that—for the first time since Holly's death—Rachel felt a glimmer of something other than pain. It was as though Holly herself was reaching out to her, telling her it was okay to go on, that she was still loved, still needed.

The session ended, but its impact remained. Rachel left feeling lighter, as if a small part of the crushing weight on her heart had lifted. The grief was still there, raw and painful, but now there was also a sense of connection—a feeling that Holly wasn't truly gone, but simply elsewhere.

In the weeks that followed, Rachel began to take small steps towards healing. She still visited Holly's room, but now it was to talk to her, to share her day, to feel her presence. She began attending grief counselling—something she had previously resisted—and found solace in the stories of others who had lost loved ones. Slowly, she began to allow herself to live again—not by leaving Holly behind, but by carrying her love and light forward into the world.

Rachel continued to see me from time to time, finding comfort in the messages relayed from Holly. Each session reminded her that her daughter's spirit was still with her—guiding her through the darkness, urging her to keep going.

It wasn't easy. There were still days when the grief felt too much to bear. But Rachel now knew she wasn't alone. Holly was with her—and that knowledge gave her the strength to carry on. In time, the thought of joining Holly no longer held the same allure. Instead, Rachel found a new purpose in living—for herself, for her son James, and for Holly, whose love would forever remain a part of her, no matter where she was.

Rachel's journey through grief was far from over, but she had found a way to keep moving forward, one step at a time—guided by her daughter's love and the hope that, one day, they would be reunited in a place free from pain and sorrow. Until then, she would live, and she would love, with Holly's spirit as her constant companion.

# Chapter Nine

## *Seeking Professional Help*

**Seeking Help After Loss: Professional and Spiritual Support**

Losing a loved one is an immensely challenging and painful experience. The grief that follows can be overwhelming, affecting every aspect of your life. While everyone's grieving process is unique, recognising when to seek specialist help and understanding where to begin can make a significant difference in navigating this difficult time. In addition, exploring spiritual support can offer comfort and guidance, adding another dimension to the healing journey.

This chapter explores how to recognise the right time to seek help, where to start, and the various forms of proficient and spiritual support available.

### Recognising the Right Time to Seek Help

Grief is a natural response to loss, and each person experiences it differently. However, certain signs may indicate it's time to seek specialised skilled support:

- **Prolonged Grief**: *If intense feelings of sadness and despair persist beyond six months with little or no improvement, qualified guidance or help may be necessary.*
- **Inability to Function**: *When grief interferes with your ability to perform daily tasks—such as working, studying, or caring for yourself and others—support can help restore balance.*
- **Emotional Numbness**: *Feeling emotionally disconnected from the world and those around you for a prolonged period may signal the need for intervention.*
- **Physical Symptoms**: *Chronic issues such as headaches, stomach problems, or significant weight changes without a medical explanation can be linked to unresolved grief.*
- **Severe Depression or Anxiety**: *Experiencing severe depressive or anxious symptoms, including thoughts of self-harm or suicide, requires immediate specialist intervention.*
- **Substance Misuse**: *Using drugs or alcohol to cope with your grief is a clear indication that both your emotional health and potential dependency need to be addressed.*

## Where to Start?

Seeking professional help while coping with grief can feel daunting. Here are some steps to help you begin:

- **Acknowledge Your Need for Support**: *The first and most crucial step is recognising that you need* *help. Seeking support is a sign of strength, not weakness.*

- **Contact Your GP**: *Your general practitioner can evaluate your overall health, rule out medical causes for your symptoms, and refer you to a mental health practitioner.*
- **Reach Out to a Mental Health Advisor**: *Psychologists, psychiatrists, and licensed counsellors specialise in grief and loss. Therapies such as cognitive behavioural therapy (CBT) have proven effective for managing complicated grief.*
- **Explore Support Groups**: *Grief support groups, often available through hospitals, community centres, or online platforms, offer a safe space to share experiences and feel less isolated.*
- **Consider Grief-Specific Counselling**: *Grief counsellors provide tailored support to help individuals navigate loss and find a path to healing.*
- **Use Online Therapy Options**: *For those unable to access in-person services, virtual therapy offers flexibility and convenience. Many licensed specialists now offer secure online sessions.*

## Types of Professional Support

A range of expert resources are available to assist you during your grieving process:

- **Individual Therapy**: *One-on-one counselling provides personalised support and coping strategies. A therapist can help you explore your emotions and address unresolved issues.*

- **Group Therapy**: *Group sessions with others experiencing similar losses can be deeply validating and comforting.*
- **Bereavement Counselling**: *These specialists help clients navigate the stages of grief, honour their loved ones, and rebuild their lives.*
- **Medication Management**: *In cases of severe anxiety or depression, a psychiatrist may recommend medication as part of a comprehensive treatment plan.*
- **Cognitive Behavioural Therapy (CBT)**: *CBT addresses negative thought patterns and behaviours, helping you build healthier coping mechanisms.*
- **Mindfulness and Relaxation Techniques**: *Many therapists incorporate mindfulness practices—such as meditation, deep breathing, and progressive muscle relaxation—to reduce stress and anxiety.*

## Exploring Spiritual Support

In addition to psychological care, many people find healing through spiritual beliefs and practices. Spiritual support can provide a sense of meaning and connection in the face of profound loss. Consider the following avenues:

- **Faith-Based Counselling**: *Many religious institutions offer counselling that blends spiritual guidance with therapeutic techniques. These counsellors can help you find comfort within your faith tradition.*

- **Prayer and Meditation**: *These practices can offer inner peace and a sense of connection to a higher power or your inner self.*
- **Spiritual Support Groups**: *Faith communities often host grief support groups, offering comfort through shared belief systems and communal support.*
- **Psychic Mediums**: *Some individuals find solace through psychic mediums who claim to communicate with the deceased, providing messages that offer comfort and a continued sense of connection.*
- **Rituals and Ceremonies**: *Participating in memorial services, lighting candles, or other meaningful rituals can foster healing, closure, and community support.*
- **Sacred Texts**: *Religious texts such as the Bible, Quran, Bhagavad Gita, or other spiritual writings may offer insights and passages that bring peace and reassurance.*
- **Spiritual Guidance**: *Spiritual leaders—such as priests, pastors, rabbis, imams, or spiritual advisors—can offer compassionate support and practical advice rooted in faith.*
- **Mind–Body Practices**: *Disciplines like yoga, tai chi, and qi gong integrate movement, mindfulness, and spiritual awareness, promoting emotional and physical healing.*
- **Nature and Solitude**: *Spending quiet time in nature can offer a profound sense of peace, grounding you in the rhythms of life and reminding you of life's continuity.*

## Taking the First Step

Initiating the process of seeking help whether professional, spiritual, or both can be challenging but is an essential part of healing. Consider these tips to support your journey:

- **Speak to Someone You Trust**: *Share your feelings with a trusted friend or family member who can offer encouragement and support.*
- **Set Manageable Goals**: *Begin with small steps, such as researching therapists, booking an initial consultation, or attending your first support group session.*
- **Be Gentle with Yourself**: *Grief does not follow a set timeline. Allow yourself to feel without judgement.*
- **Remain Open**: *Counselling and spiritual support may uncover deep emotions. Stay open to the process, knowing that growth often comes from discomfort.*
- **Keep a Journal**: *Writing can help you process emotions, reflect on your progress, and identify recurring patterns or needs.*
- **Explore Spiritual Practices**: *Try different spiritual activities to see what resonates—whether prayer, meditation, or mindful movement, find what brings you solace.*

Consulting a specialist or taking spiritual help after the loss of a loved one is a brave and vital step towards healing. By recognising when to reach out, understanding your options, and embracing the support available, you can find the strength to carry on.

Remember, it is entirely okay to ask for help. A holistic approach combining psychological and spiritual care can lead to profound healing, helping you rediscover peace, purpose, and connection in the midst of your grief.

## Mike's Story

Mike had always been a pragmatic man, relying on logic and reason to navigate life's challenges. But when his beloved daughter succumbed to a terminal illness, his world was shattered, leaving him engulfed in an overwhelming sea of grief and helplessness. Unsure where to turn for support and finding little solace in conventional methods, he confided in a close friend about his despair. Recognising Mike's profound need for comfort and closure, the friend referred him to me suggesting that a spiritual connection might offer the guidance he so desperately needed. Sceptical but desperate for relief, Mike decided to give it a try, hoping to reconnect with his daughter and to find reassurance that she was at peace.

Through our sessions, Mike received messages that resonated deeply with his memories and experiences of his daughter, bringing a sense of her presence and confirmation that she was no longer suffering. The messages were intimate and specific, touching on personal memories and shared moments that only his daughter could have known. This spiritual experience brought Mike a profound sense of comfort, making him feel that his daughter was still with him in spirit watching over and guiding him.

This connection enabled Mike to come to terms with his loss, providing the solace and closure he needed to move forward with his life. He found peace in the knowledge that his daughter's spirit remained close, helping him navigate his grief and begin to heal. Inspired by this experience, he started re-engaging with the world around him. He resumed hobbies he had long abandoned, reconnected with old friends, and even began volunteering at a local children's hospital in his daughter's memory. Through this journey of spiritual healing, Mike discovered a renewed sense of purpose and a reason to keep going, gradually rebuilding his life and finding joy once more amidst the sorrow.

## Losing a Parent

Losing a parent is one of the most deeply felt and heart-wrenching experiences one can endure. When my father passed away, it was like standing on solid ground one moment and free-falling the next. The pain was both immediate and overwhelming, touching every aspect of my life. My father had been a cornerstone of my existence—a constant source of support, wisdom, and unconditional love. His absence left a void that seemed impossible to fill. I felt utterly alone in the world.

In the days that followed his passing, I was swept up in a whirlwind of emotion. Shock, disbelief, and an all-consuming sadness dominated my every waking moment. Friends and family rallied around me, offering their support and condolences. While their presence was comforting, there remained an inexplicable hollowness within me that nothing seemed to soothe. The grief was all-encompassing, impairing my ability to eat, sleep, or think clearly.

Despite the outpouring of support, I struggled to articulate the depth of my pain. I felt isolated in my sorrow, as though no one could truly grasp the magnitude of my loss. As days turned into weeks, I noticed a strain in my relationships. Well-intentioned advice and attempts at consolation often felt inadequate or misplaced. Conversations that were meant to comfort sometimes left me feeling even more alone.

One particularly difficult night, when sleep continued to evade me and memories of my father flooded my mind, I realised I needed more than just the support of loved ones. The grief was too profound, the pain too deep, to navigate alone or even with the help of those closest to me. I needed a different kind of support, one that could offer a new perspective and deeper healing.

This realisation was not immediate but came gradually through weeks of internal struggle. I began to notice troubling patterns in my behaviour. I was withdrawing socially, avoiding even the closest of friends, and losing interest in things I once enjoyed. My physical health was also deteriorating—I had lost a considerable amount of weight, and restful sleep had become rare.

One morning, after another sleepless night, I opened up to a close friend about my ongoing struggle. He listened with empathy and suggested I explore alternative forms of support. He mentioned that his cousin had found great solace in visiting a psychic medium after losing a loved one, and that the experience had brought a unique sense of comfort and closure. Having already visited a spiritualist church and occasionally felt my father's presence, this seemed like a natural next step for me.

I began researching psychic mediums and their practices. I discovered that many people had found peace through connecting with mediums, who claimed to communicate with the spirits of the departed. The testimonials were compelling. People described renewed feelings of connection and emotional relief after their sessions. I began to see this as an opportunity to bridge the gap between my grief and my father's spirit, and to find the closure I had not been able to achieve through traditional means.

Encouraged by my findings and the stories I had read, I decided to take the first step. I reached out to the psychic medium my friend had recommended. She was highly praised for her compassionate nature and the accuracy and depth of her readings. Despite my low mood, I felt a glimmer of hope that this might be the path to healing.

Booking the appointment was an emotional experience in itself. As I dialled the number and spoke to the medium's assistant, I felt a mixture of anticipation and anxiety. Was this truly the right decision? Could I really find the comfort I was seeking? The assistant was kind and reassuring, explaining that many people felt the same before their first session.

On the day of the appointment, I arrived at the medium's home with a heavy heart and a mind full of questions. The room was serene—filled with calming scents and soft music. The medium welcomed me warmly, her presence instantly putting me at ease. She explained the process and asked if there were any particular questions or messages I hoped to receive.

As the session began, I was struck by her gentle manner and the tranquillity of the space. She described my father's personality and shared intimate details only someone close to him could have known. Her words brought tears to my eyes, confirming that my father was present in spirit. She conveyed messages of love and comfort, telling me he was at peace and watching over me. She also acknowledged that I had already sensed his presence, which brought me even greater comfort.

That session was transformative. For the first time since my father's passing, I felt a genuine sense of connection and closure. The messages I received gave me immense comfort, helping me understand that his spirit remained with me, guiding and protecting me. This awareness brought a profound peace that I had been unable to find through conventional avenues.

In the days that followed, I noticed a marked shift in my emotional state. The weight of grief began to lift, replaced by a sense of calm and acceptance. I felt more at ease with my father's passing, reassured by the knowledge that his spirit was still part of my life. With this renewed perspective, I began to re-engage with the world, gradually finding joy in activities I had once loved.

Seeking help from a psychic medium proved to be a pivotal moment in my journey through grief. It offered a unique form of spiritual healing that complemented the emotional support of friends and family. This alternative approach provided the closure and comfort I so desperately needed, allowing me to come to terms with my loss and rediscover a sense of purpose.

As I continue to move through life without my father, I remain deeply grateful for the guidance and healing I received from that experience. It taught me the importance of exploring all avenues of support, especially when traditional methods fall short. Grief is an intensely personal journey, and finding the right kind of help is essential. For me, seeking alternative support was the key to healing—honouring my father's memory and living a fuller, more meaningful life.

# Chapter Ten

## *Stories of Hope and Healing*

### Sara's Story

Sara had always been inseparable from her mother, Lily. They shared everything: secrets, laughter, dreams, and an unbreakable bond that formed the cornerstone of Sara's life. Lily was her confidante, greatest supporter, and best friend. When Lily was diagnosed with a terminal illness, Sara's world was shaken to its core. Despite the grim prognosis, the two faced the challenge together, cherishing every moment they had left.

The day Lily passed away was the darkest of Sara's life. The grief was immediate and overwhelming, a heavy blanket that smothered her spirit. She withdrew from the world, finding little solace in the well-meaning words of comfort from friends and family. Every room in their house echoed with Lily's absence, and Sara struggled to find her footing in a world that now felt empty and unfamiliar.

For months, Sara moved through her days in a fog of sadness and disbelief. She went through the motions at work, barely engaging with colleagues or clients, and spent her evenings alone, surrounded by memories that brought both comfort and pain. Her friends grew increasingly concerned, urging her to seek help, but Sara felt paralysed by her grief—unable to imagine a future without her mother.

One afternoon, while sorting through some of Lily's belongings, Sara found a journal her mother had kept during her illness. In it, Lily had written about her hopes and dreams for Sara, her deep love for her daughter, and her wish for Sara to find happiness and peace after she was gone. Reading her mother's words, Sara felt a glimmer of hope for the first time since Lily's death. It was as if Lily were reaching out from the beyond, urging her to live fully once again.

Encouraged by this sense of connection, Sara decided to take a friend's advice and attend a grief support group. She was nervous at first, unsure of what to expect, but as she listened to others share their stories of loss and healing, she realised she was not alone. The group became a sanctuary—a safe space where she could express her pain and feel understood by others who had walked a similar path.

Through the support group, Sara met a woman named Anna, who had lost her husband a few years earlier. Anna had a calm, reassuring presence and a wisdom born from her own journey through grief. They quickly became friends, and Anna introduced Sara to healing practices that had helped her—such as yoga, meditation, and journalling. Sara found that these activities offered a way to process her emotions and gradually begin to heal her wounded heart.

One day, Anna mentioned a psychic medium she had visited after her husband's death. She described how the session had brought her comfort and a sense of connection. Intrigued but sceptical, Sara decided to give it a try. She booked an appointment, hoping it might bring her peace.

The medium, a kind and empathetic woman named Grace, welcomed Sara warmly. As the session began, Grace conveyed messages that seemed to come from Lily. These messages were filled with love and reassurance, touching on specific memories and shared moments that only Lily would have known. Sara felt a profound sense of her mother's presence, as if Lily were sitting right beside her, offering comfort and guidance.

The experience with Grace was life-changing. It gave Sara a deep sense of closure and connection, affirming that Lily's spirit was still with her watching over and supporting her. This spiritual encounter gave Sara the strength to begin rebuilding her life, embracing new opportunities and cherishing memories without being overwhelmed by them.

Over time, Sara's grief began to soften, making space for moments of joy and hope. She resumed hobbies she had abandoned, reconnected with friends, and began volunteering at a local hospice, supporting families going through similar experiences. Through this work, she found a renewed sense of purpose and a meaningful way to honour Lily's memory.

Sara's journey through grief was not linear—there were still days of sadness and longing. However, the combination of skilled support, spiritual connection, and the loving community she discovered helped her to heal and grow. She learned that healing is a process—one that requires patience, compassion, and the willingness to seek and accept help.

In the end, Sara found a way to live fully once more, carrying her mother's love in her heart as a source of strength and inspiration. She discovered that hope and healing are possible—even after the deepest loss—and that life, though forever changed, can still be beautiful and meaningful.

## Alex's Story

The doorbell rang, and a young man stepped inside my home. He appeared to be in his late twenties, with a weary expression that spoke of sleepless nights and a heart burdened with grief. His eyes were dull and lifeless.

Alex had been hesitant to come, feeling a strange mix of hope and scepticism. He had heard about me, and my ability to connect with those who had passed beyond the veil. He needed answers—or perhaps just a sign—something to guide him through the dense fog of despair that had enveloped his life. I had seen this look many times before: the look of someone on the edge, grasping for something to hold onto in a world that had suddenly become unbearably empty.

"Please, have a seat," I said gently, motioning to the chair across from me.

Alex sat down, wringing his hands nervously. He took a deep breath and looked up at me, his voice barely above a whisper. "I've lost someone… someone very important to me."

"Please don't tell me anything yet. I'll just try to connect with my spirit guide." I responded.

I felt a subtle shift in the room—a familiar sensation that often accompanied the presence of spirits. I closed my eyes, reaching out with my senses, feeling the energy around me. The air seemed to thicken, and a gentle warmth settled over me, like a comforting embrace.

After a moment, I opened my eyes, now gazing beyond Alex as if seeing something only I could perceive.

"Jeremy is here," I said softly. "He's been watching over you—he's worried about you."

Alex's breath caught in his throat, tears welling in his eyes. "He is? Does he… does he know how much I miss him?"

I nodded, my voice calm and steady. "He knows. He wants you to know that he loves you deeply and that he's at peace. He remembers the good times—the love you shared. He still feels that love, even now."

A tear slid down Alex's cheek. "I can't bear this pain. I just want to be with him again."

The room grew warmer, and I sensed a strong, protective presence. Jeremy's spirit was close—projecting a message filled with urgency and love.

"Jeremy wants you to understand that your time here isn't over," I said with gentle firmness. "He knows how much you're hurting, but he wants you to live—to find happiness again. He believes in you and wants you to carry on, not just for him, but for yourself. He says, 'Your life is worth living, Alex. You still have so much love to give, so much more to experience.'"

Alex shook his head, overwhelmed by emotion. "I don't know if I can do it without him."

Jeremy's energy grew more insistent, almost pleading.

"He says you can. He wants you to promise that you'll try. He doesn't want you to end your life—he wants you to honour the love you shared by living fully and finding joy again. He'll be waiting for you—but not yet. He doesn't want you to rush to him."

Tears streamed down Alex's face as he listened to Jeremy's words. The despair that had consumed him began to ease, replaced by a bittersweet mix of sorrow and hope.

"Thank you," Alex whispered, his voice breaking. "Thank you, Jeremy. And thank you, John. I… I think I can try. For him. For us."

He explained, "My partner, Jeremy… we were together for eight years. And now… he's gone. I couldn't cope. I needed to know if he was okay—if he understood why I wanted to join him."

Alex told me he had contemplated ending his life to escape the torment of living without his beloved partner. But after hearing Jeremy speak so clearly insisting that he live his life to the fullest Alex assured me he would do his best to honour that wish.

I nodded. "You're never truly alone, Alex. Love transcends even death. Remember that and take it one day at a time. Jeremy will always be a part of you, and he'll always be watching over you."

As Alex left, the weight of his grief seemed a little lighter. He still had a long journey ahead one filled with healing and rediscovery but for the first time since Jeremy's passing, he felt a spark of hope. He knew it would be hard, but he was willing to try to live the life Jeremy wanted for him.

## Margaret's Story

A woman named Margaret booked a session with me. She was known among her friends and neighbours for her warm smile and kind heart, but for the past year, her smile had been tinged with sorrow. Margaret had lost her husband, Dave, to a sudden illness. They had shared twenty beautiful years together, filled with laughter, adventure, and love.

Dave's death had left a void in Margaret's life—a shadow that followed her everywhere. The house they had made a home now felt empty, the garden they had lovingly tended was overgrown with weeds, and the laughter they once shared had been replaced by an echoing silence. Despite the love and support from friends and family, Margaret struggled to find joy in a world without him.

One sunny morning, as Margaret sat on the porch sipping her coffee, she felt a gentle breeze carrying the salty scent of the sea. It reminded her of the times she and Dave would walk along the beach, collecting seashells and watching the waves. She closed her eyes, feeling the warmth of the sun on her face, and took a deep breath. For the first time in a long while, she felt a flicker of something she hadn't known in months—hope.

That day, she decided to take a walk along the shore. She slipped on her sandals, grabbed her sunhat, and set off for the beach. The sand was warm beneath her feet, and the rhythmic sound of the waves was soothing. As she walked, she noticed a group of children laughing and playing—building sandcastles and chasing seagulls. Their joy was infectious, and Margaret found herself smiling.

Further along the beach, she came across a man painting a seascape on an easel. He had a friendly face and wore a blue cap that shaded his eyes. The canvas depicted the very scene in front of them—the turquoise waters, gentle waves, and a bright blue sky.

"That's beautiful, Margaret said, stopping to admire the painting.

The man looked up and smiled. "Thank you. I'm Mark," he said, extending his hand.

"Margaret," she replied, shaking it.

They chatted for a while, and Margaret learned that Mark was a local artist who often came to the beach for inspiration. He had moved to the area a few years earlier, drawn by the town's peaceful beauty and vibrant community. As they talked, Margaret felt a connection forming—a lightness she hadn't experienced in a long time.

Days turned into weeks, and Margaret and Mark continued to meet on the beach. They shared stories, laughed together, and found comfort in each other's company. Mark was kind and understanding, never pressing Margaret to talk about her grief, but always ready to listen when she needed to. He, too, had experienced loss, and together they found solace in their shared understanding of life's fragility.

One day, Mark invited Margaret to join him for a picnic at the town's annual summer festival. The festival was a lively event, with music, dancing, and food stalls offering delicious local treats. Margaret hesitated at first, unsure if she was ready to embrace life again but Mark's enthusiasm was contagious.

At the festival, Margaret felt a sense of community she hadn't known in a long time. The vibrant colours, the laughter, and the music filled her heart with warmth. As the sun set, Mark took her hand and led her to the dance floor. They danced under fairy lights, surrounded by couples and families. For the first time in what felt like forever, Margaret allowed herself to be swept up in the moment, laughing and twirling with Mark.

As the night came to a close, Mark walked Margaret home. They stood on her porch, the moonlight casting a soft glow over them. Margaret felt a mix of emotions gratitude, joy, and a trace of guilt. She looked at Mark, his eyes kind and understanding, and said, "I haven't felt this happy in such a long time. It feels strange, but... good."

Mark smiled gently. "It's okay to feel happy again, Margaret. It's okay to move forward. Dave would want that for you."

Margaret had come to see me because she wanted to be sure that Dave was at peace and that he would be happy for her to move on. She was struggling with mixed emotions—sadness, guilt, and the happiness that Mark had now brought into her life.

I passed on the messages that Dave had for her—that he *wanted her to live her life, that he was okay and no longer suffering*, and that he was happy to see her smile again.

Tears welled up in Margaret's eyes—not from sorrow, but from the profound relief that it was true. Dave had always been her greatest supporter, her source of strength. He would want her to find joy and love again, to live life fully. She felt a deep sense of peace, realising that moving on didn't mean forgetting—it meant honouring the love they had shared by living her life to the fullest.

In the months that followed, Margaret and Mark grew closer. They explored the town together, painted, laughed, and dreamed of new adventures. Margaret reopened the garden, planting new flowers that bloomed in vivid colours—a symbol of her renewed hope and the beauty of new beginnings.

Margaret knew she would always carry Dave in her heart, but she also understood that life still had so much to offer. With Mark by her side, she felt excited about the future—a new chapter filled with love, friendship, and endless possibilities.

As she stood in her garden, watching the flowers sway in the gentle breeze, Margaret smiled—a true, heartfelt smile. She knew that, no matter what, she would be okay. She had found hope again—a new dawn in her life—and she was ready to embrace it with open arms.

## Reece's Story

Reece walked in to see me with a look that said he'd rather be anywhere else. He was tall, with a strong build that suggested he was used to facing things head-on, and a demeanour that radiated scepticism. He glanced around my modest space, taking in the soft lighting, the shelves filled with crystals, and the faint scent of sage lingering in the air. His eyes finally settled on me, and I could see the doubt etched into his face.

"My wife booked this," he said, almost defensively, as if justifying his presence. "I'm not really into... this sort of thing."

I nodded, offering a warm smile. "I understand, Reece. Many people come in with reservations. I'm John Hughes, and my goal is simply to help, however I can. If you're open to it, we can explore whatever you feel comfortable with."

He gave a reluctant nod and sat down, his posture stiff and guarded. I could sense the walls he had built around himself—thick and impenetrable. It was clear this wouldn't be an easy session, but I'd encountered this before. Patience and persistence would be key.

We began the session, and I started with some gentle observations—things I was picking up on: his restlessness, the weight he seemed to carry on his shoulders. But each time I made a statement or passed on a message I received, he either dismissed it or responded with a noncommittal grunt. There was no opening, no crack in his armour. The session ended with Reece as closed off as he'd been when he walked in, and I could tell he was eager to leave.

"Thanks," he said curtly as he stood up. "But I don't think this is for me."

I smiled again, unfazed by his reaction. "I'm here if you ever feel like coming back. Sometimes it takes a few sessions to really connect."

To my surprise, Reece did return—about a month later. He looked just as sceptical as before, but something had shifted. Perhaps it was curiosity, or maybe his wife's gentle insistence, but he came back—reluctantly. We went through the same motions, and once again he resisted, deflecting anything I said with logic and reason.

It wasn't until the third session that I noticed a subtle shift. Reece began to speak a little more, though still guardedly. He mentioned his job—a high-pressure role at a construction firm—and the constant expectation to be strong and unshakeable. I sensed there was something deeper beneath the surface, but I knew better than to push too hard.

Over the next few sessions, we continued peeling back the layers. I passed on what I was receiving—messages, impressions, fragments of energy. It was like peeling an onion, one thin layer at a time. Reece began to open up more about his life: his childhood, his relationship with his father, and the fear of failure that haunted him despite his outward success. But even as he shared these things, he remained hesitant to believe there was anything beyond the physical world.

"Look, John," he said during one session, frustration creeping into his voice. "I get that this works for some people, but I just don't see how any of this is real. I'm a facts-and-figures guy. I need proof."

I nodded, understanding where he was coming from. "I'm not here to convince you of anything, Reece. This is your journey. I'm just here to guide you, to help you find your own truth. Perhaps it's not about believing in the supernatural, but about understanding yourself better."

He mulled that over, and for the first time, I saw a flicker of consideration in his eyes.

It took many more sessions before Reece's barriers began to truly crumble. There were moments of frustration, times when he nearly walked away for good, and occasions where he'd take one step forward only to fall two steps back. But gradually, the walls he had built around himself began to weaken.

In one particularly intense session, Reece finally let down his guard completely. He spoke about the pain he had carried for years—the unresolved grief of losing his mother when he was young. He admitted he had buried it so deeply, believing that ignoring it made him stronger. As he spoke, I could feel the energy shift in the room. It was as though a heavy burden was being lifted from him, piece by piece.

Tears welled up in his eyes, and he made no effort to hide them. "I've been so scared," he whispered, his voice trembling. "Scared of feeling this, of facing it."

I reached out, offering reassurance. "It's okay, Reece. You don't have to carry it alone anymore. You've taken the first step, and that's always the hardest."

From that point on, our sessions took on a different tone. Reece became more open, more willing to explore the parts of himself he had kept hidden for so long. He began to understand that the energy we were tapping into wasn't about magic or mysticism, but about the deep emotional currents running through his life. It was about connecting with himself in a way he had never allowed before.

He eventually admitted to me that he had returned because he couldn't deny the accuracy of the information I had shared during his first visit—and the sessions that followed. He had wanted a logical explanation, and when only one remained, he felt compelled to come back.

By the time we reached the end of our journey together, Reece had transformed in ways he never imagined. He hadn't become a sudden believer in the supernatural, but he had learned to trust his intuition, to listen to his inner voice, and to confront the emotions he had locked away for so long. He was lighter, freer, and finally at peace with the parts of himself he had once feared to face.

As he shook my hand during our final session, he looked me in the eye and said, "Thank you, John. I didn't think I'd get anything out of this, but you helped me see things in a way I never could before."

I smiled, feeling a deep sense of satisfaction. "It was all within you, Reece. I just helped you find it."

And with that, Reece walked out of my office for the last time—not burdened by the scepticism that had once defined him, but with a newfound understanding of himself and the world around him.

# Chapter Eleven

## *The Unthinkable Loss – Losing a Child and Learning to Breathe Again*

There is something inherently unnatural about a parent outliving their child. It defies the quiet expectations we hold in our hearts—the belief that we will guide them, protect them, and grow old while they bloom into the full story of who they were meant to be. But when that story is cut short, you're left holding all the pages that will never be written. And the silence of those unwritten chapters can feel louder than anything you've ever known.

### When Everything Stops

The first days after the loss are a blur—suspended between shock and unbearable sorrow. People come with kind eyes and casserole dishes, offering words that don't land. They mean well, but nothing can reach you. You're in another world now, a place where time is distorted and every breath feels like an effort. You may smile out of politeness or nod when someone says, "They're in a better place," but inside, there's a scream so deep you're not sure you'll ever return from it.

You may wonder if you're going mad. You might search their room for a trace of their scent. You may talk to them in the dead of night or imagine them sitting on the edge of your bed. You're not losing your mind. You're grieving. And grief after the loss of a child is neither linear nor logical—it's tidal, crashing over you in unpredictable waves. Some days you may feel numb. Other days you collapse under the weight of a toy left behind, a song they loved, or the sound of a child's laughter in a supermarket aisle.

## Trying to Make Sense of the Unimaginable

At some point, the question begins to rise—Why? Why them? Why now? Why would life, God, the universe—whatever you believe in—take someone so innocent, so full of potential?

The truth is, there may never be a satisfying answer.

Trying to make sense of such loss isn't about finding a neat explanation—it's about surviving the questions. It's about slowly learning how to live with the mystery. For some, faith provides a framework. For others, it's a quiet turning inward, a search for connection that exists beyond words. You may begin to notice signs—feathers, dreams, flickering lights, an unexplained warmth. These are not coincidences. They are comfort. They are reminders, subtle and sacred, that love does not end with death.

## The Spirit of a Child

There is something pure and powerful about the spirit of a child. Many who have experienced such loss speak of how their child seemed to 'visit' them—sometimes in dreams so vivid, you wake up feeling as though you truly held them again. Other times, it's in gentler ways: a breeze that feels like a hug, a toy that moves inexplicably, a thought that enters your mind as if spoken in their voice.

You might question these things at first, but as time passes, you begin to understand: your child has not left you—not completely. The physical form may be gone, yes, but their energy—their soul—is still very much alive. And sometimes, in the quiet spaces between grief, you feel them. You just know.

They are near. Watching. Loving. Waiting.

## The Living and the Loving

In time—and it may take months, years, or longer—you may find that grief doesn't leave, but it does soften. It becomes something you carry, a sacred weight that walks beside you. You may laugh again, and that laughter may sting with guilt at first. But your child would want that joy for you. They were made of love, and they live now through your loving.

You begin to understand that healing is not betrayal. Smiling is not forgetting. You carry them in every step, in every breath, in every act of kindness you bring into the world. Their name may not be spoken aloud as often, but their presence is stitched into the very fabric of your being.

You never "move on"—you move forward. And that difference is everything.

## A Note to the Broken-hearted

If you are reading this and you have lost a child, know this: you are not alone. Though it may feel like it, you have joined a sacred circle of parents who carry invisible scars, who continue breathing when it feels impossible, who wake up every day learning how to live without—but also with—the spirit of a child who changed them forever.

You are doing the impossible. And that is more than enough.

Let no one rush your grief. Let no one diminish your pain. Let no one tell you how to heal. This is your journey, and your child—your beautiful, beloved child—is with you still.

In every sunrise. In every heartbeat. In every moment of grace when you choose to keep going. And when you are ready, you may find yourself speaking to them not with tears, but with love. Not asking, *Why did you leave?*

But whispering, *I feel you nearby.*

## Priya and Naz's Story

Priya and Naz contacted me for a reading via Zoom; they were both deep in grief and overwhelmed by their loss. I gave them readings on several occasions, bringing through messages from their child, and this became a part of the way they navigated their grief.

Priya and Naz were a loving couple who lived in the vibrant city of Melbourne, Australia. They were known for their warmth and the eclectic café they owned, named *Elysium*—a favourite gathering place for locals. The café, filled with lush greenery, cosy nooks, and the comforting aroma of freshly brewed coffee and homemade pastries, was more than just a business. It was a labour of love, a reflection of their shared passion for creating a space where people could find comfort and joy.

Their happiness was magnified by the arrival of their beautiful daughter, Zara. Zara was a radiant child, blessed with a contagious laugh and an insatiable curiosity. She brought endless joy to Priya and Naz, filling their lives with love and laughter. However, their happiness was shattered when Zara fell ill with a rare and aggressive disease. Despite their best efforts, and the support of the community, Zara passed away at the tender age of four.

The loss of Zara was an unimaginable blow. Priya and Naz were devastated, and their once-vibrant world seemed to lose all its colour. The café, which had been a place of joy, now felt empty and cold. They closed it temporarily, unable to summon the strength to face their customers or the memories that lingered in every corner.

For weeks, they withdrew into their grief, struggling to find a way forward. The pain was overwhelming, and the silence in their home served as a constant reminder of their loss. They felt unmoored, their hearts heavy with sorrow.

One day, while cleaning Zara's room, they discovered a small sketchbook filled with her drawings. Among the pages were pictures of flowers, smiling suns, and a family of stick figures—Priya, Naz, and Zara—standing beneath a rainbow. On the final pages, Zara had drawn a garden filled with colourful blooms, with a message in her shaky handwriting: *"A garden makes everything happy."*

Reading those words, Priya and Naz felt a flicker of inspiration. Zara had adored the garden at their café, often helping to water the plants and picking flowers to give to customers. They realised that the garden Zara had envisioned could become a way to honour her memory and bring light back into their lives.

With a renewed sense of purpose, Priya and Naz decided to reopen Elysium with a new vision. They transformed the café's courtyard into a beautiful garden, filled with the most vivid and striking flowers and plants they could find. They named it *Zara's Garden*—a tribute to their beloved daughter. The garden became the heart of the café, a sanctuary where people could find peace and solace.

To further honour Zara's memory, Priya and Naz launched a community initiative called *Blooming Hearts*. They partnered with local schools, inviting children to plant flowers and learn about gardening. They also established a small charity fund, donating a portion of the café's proceeds to support research into childhood illnesses. The initiative aimed to share Zara's love of nature and bring joy to other children and families.

As word spread about *Zara's Garden* and the *Blooming Hearts* initiative, the community rallied around Priya and Naz. Customers returned not only for the delicious food and warm atmosphere but also for the hope and healing the café now represented. The garden became a symbol of resilience and love—a place where people could remember, recover, and reconnect.

Priya and Naz found comfort in tending the garden. It felt as though they were nurturing Zara's spirit, keeping her memory alive in every blooming flower and every smile from a child planting their first seed. The garden became a space for reflection, where they could recall joyful moments with Zara and draw strength from their love for her.

One sunny afternoon, as they watched a group of children planting flowers, Priya turned to Naz, her eyes glistening with tears.

"She would have loved this," she whispered. Naz nodded, a gentle smile on his lips. "She's here with us," he said, gazing around at the garden that had brought joy to so many. "In every flower, every laugh, and every act of kindness, Zara's spirit lives on."

Through their pain, Priya and Naz had discovered a way to transform grief into something beautiful and meaningful. They had created a space where their daughter's memory could inspire happiness and hope in others. In *Zara's Garden*, they found that while nothing could replace their beloved child, they could honour her memory by spreading love and compassion.

The café, once a place of sorrow, had become a sanctuary of healing and joy. And as the flowers blossomed and the children played, Priya and Naz found peace—knowing that Zara's legacy would continue to bloom and touch the hearts of many.

# Chapter Twelve

## *Grief, Spirit Messages, and the Sensitivity of Children*

Grief has a way of altering time. Some moments stretch endlessly, while others collapse into a blur of disbelief. When someone we love passes away, the world keeps turning, but something deep within us shifts irrevocably. In the quiet, aching spaces that grief creates, many begin to notice things they hadn't before—a gentle nudge, a flicker of light, a dream that feels far too vivid to ignore.

### The Language of Spirit

Across cultures and spiritual traditions, there is a shared belief: our loved ones do not simply vanish when they die. Instead, they move into another realm of existence—one without physical form, yet filled with presence, love, and consciousness. This realm is often called the Spirit World, the Other Side, or simply "home".

A spirit often communicates through subtle means. These messages aren't always spoken words—they come as symbols, synchronicities, feelings, dreams, or a sudden sense that someone is near. You might catch the scent of your grandmother's perfume in an empty room, find a feather in an unlikely place, or hear a song on the radio that held special meaning between you and someone who has passed.

These are not coincidences. They are messages—gentle reminders that love does not end with death. Spirit reaches out not to haunt us, but to comfort and reassure us that they are at peace, and that we are never truly alone.

## The Tender Hearts of Children

Children are naturally attuned to the unseen. Unburdened by scepticism or societal conditioning, they sense energy and presence in a raw, intuitive way. After a loved one passes, it's not uncommon for children to describe seeing them, hearing their voice, or playing with them in dreams. These experiences are often so matter-of-fact that adults may overlook their significance.

A child might say, "Grandpa told me not to be sad," or recall a visit from a beloved pet who passed away. These are not fabrications. Children often act as bridges between the physical and spiritual realms—especially in times of grief, when the veil between worlds seems thinner. Rather than dismiss these experiences, it is healing to honour them. Ask your child open-ended, gentle questions such as:

- *"What did they say?"*
- *"How did you feel?"*
- *"Was it a dream, or were you awake?"*

These conversations not only validate the child's experience but also open a door to deeper healing for the whole family. In fact, messages shared by children can sometimes carry a wisdom beyond their years—as if the spirit world is speaking through them with clarity and purity.

## Grief as a Sacred Portal

Grief, though deeply painful, can also be a spiritual threshold. In our most broken moments, our hearts are often more open—vulnerable enough to receive what we might have otherwise missed. The paradox of loss is that it can also mark the beginning of a deeper spiritual awareness—one that tunes in to signs, dreams, and feelings that hint at the soul's continued existence.

Many people report feeling "guided" or protected in the weeks or months following a death. This too may be a form of communication. Spirit knows how to reach us—through our memories, our senses, our intuition, and the quiet miracles that appear when we least expect them.

## Supporting the Connection

If you wish to connect with a loved one who has passed, begin by quieting the mind and opening the heart. Grief often creates noise, comprising waves of sorrow, guilt, and longing. But beneath that turmoil lies stillness and within that stillness, spirit often waits.

Here are gentle ways to invite connection:

- *Create a sacred space in your home with photos or cherished objects.*
- *Write a letter to your loved one. Express what's in your heart. Then sit quietly, and allow any impressions to come.*
- *Pay attention to your dreams—they are a favourite avenue for spiritual messages.*
- *Encourage children to share or draw their experiences, no matter how unusual they seem.*

Above all, trust your experience. Your mind may doubt, but your soul always knows.

# Chapter Thirteen

## *There Is No Required Waiting Period For Love*

Grief doesn't follow rules. It doesn't read psychology textbooks or conform to neat five-stage models. It arrives uninvited—sometimes all at once, sometimes in waves—and often demands more from us than we ever thought we could give.

One of the most common myths about grief is this: You need to wait. Wait to cry. Wait to talk about it. Wait to move on.

For many, this myth extends into the spiritual realm as well. You might have heard:

"Don't rush into seeing a medium."

"You need time before you make contact."

"It's too soon."

But here's what I want you to know: there is no such thing as "too soon" when it comes to seeking connection.

You don't need to wait for some invisible window of "readiness" to open. If your heart is calling out, that is enough. If you're feeling the pull to reach out—through prayer, meditation, or visiting a psychic medium—that pull is valid.

Grief isn't linear, and neither is healing.

If your loved one meant the world to you in life, why should your desire to connect with them in death be something to postpone?

Some people feel called to speak with a medium the very next day. Others wait months or even years. But it's not about the calendar—it's about the need. If your grief feels too loud, too raw, too painful to carry alone, it's okay to seek help—even if that help comes in the form of spiritual support.

You may cry. You may doubt. You may feel sceptical even as your heart begins to open. That's okay. In fact, it's entirely normal.

Let go of the idea that you must be "ready" in some formal, defined way.

Grief doesn't wait. And neither does love.

**First, let's dispel a common fear:** you don't need to be a "believer" for a psychic or medium to offer something meaningful. Grief isn't a religion. Connection doesn't require blind faith. It simply asks for curiosity, presence, and willingness.

When you enter a reading—whether in person, online, or by phone—remember:

- *You don't have to say much. A good medium will lead with sensitivity and insight, not probing questions.*
- *You might not hear what you expected. Sometimes what comes through is subtle—a shared phrase, a forgotten detail, or a quiet feeling of peace. It's not always thunder. Often, it's a whisper.*
- *You're allowed to doubt. Mediums aren't there to erase your grief or replace your loss. They are there to offer connection—however it may arrive.*

Many people walk away not with definitive answers, but with a sense of relief. Not because every detail was perfect, but because they felt something—a shift, a presence, a warmth they hadn't expected.

Trust the experience. Trust yourself. Even if you leave with more questions, you may also leave with a little more space to breathe.

## Signs and Synchronicities

Here's something almost no one talks about—Once you open yourself to connection, signs often start appearing. And they don't always wait for a reading.

- *A favourite song on the radio at just the right moment*
- *A flickering light with no explanation*
- *A scent that suddenly fills the room, then vanishes*
- *A dream that feels too vivid to be "just a dream"*

These moments are easy to dismiss. But what if you didn't?

What if you paused and received them—not as proof, but as presence?

Not all signs will be grand. Many are subtle.

You might not get a blinking neon light saying, "I'm still here," but you might feel your heart lift when you see a butterfly, hear a familiar joke, or find their handwriting tucked away in an old drawer.

The more we soften into awareness, the more we begin to notice.

Signs don't scream at you—most are whispers, easily missed. And often, that's all we need. So pay attention. Be open to receive.

## Final Thoughts

Grief is love with nowhere to go. But when we allow ourselves to consider that the bond continues—that love moves beyond the body and survives death—grief becomes not just sorrow, but sacred listening.

Children can teach us so much in this space. Their openness reminds us that spirit is always nearby, just waiting to be noticed.

Let the veil be thin. Let your heart be open. Love always finds a way home.

## John's Note:

A few years after losing my father, my mother-in-law passed away. Her death was so unexpected that the entire family came together, united in shock and disbelief. She was the second deeply close person we had lost, and her passing left a vast, unfillable void in our lives. My wife was devastated, and nothing I said or did could ease her pain.

After a few months, I decided to take her to the same psychic I had visited myself, hoping it might help her come to terms with the loss of her mother or at least bring some comfort. While we were there, I felt as though I was also receiving messages meant for my wife. I felt slightly disoriented, unsure how to pass on the information without causing more distress.

The days that followed were a whirlwind of confusion and curiosity. I began experiencing phenomena I couldn't explain, knowing things before they happened, sensing emotions that weren't mine, and feeling drawn to certain people and places without understanding why. It was both exhilarating and unsettling. I couldn't shake the sense that something extraordinary was unfolding—something I needed to understand.

Determined to make sense of it, I returned to the medium alone. She welcomed me with a knowing smile, as if she had been expecting me. Over several sessions, she guided me through the process of channelling this energy, teaching me how to meditate, focus, and listen to the subtle whispers of the universe. It was as though a door had opened within me, revealing a world that had always existed just out of sight.

I had been in a serious accident some years earlier and had a similar experience—hearing messages and seeing people who had passed away. I once spoke to my mother about it, and she told me that my great-great-grandmother had been a particularly well-known psychic medium in her time. Perhaps I had inherited her abilities. Looking back, I realise the gift had always been there; I just hadn't known how to understand or manage it.

Gradually, I learned to control and refine my abilities. I discovered how to quiet my mind, tune in to the energy around me, and trust the messages I was receiving. It was like learning a new language—one that required patience, discipline, and, above all, faith in the unseen. The more I practised, the stronger the connection became. I could feel the energy flowing through me, a powerful force that was both humbling and empowering.

In time, I began offering readings to others, starting with close friends and family. The validations came quickly, their astonishment matching my own. I knew things I had no logical way of knowing, connected with spirits who brought comfort and closure to those who sought my help. What began as a vague curiosity blossomed into a profound sense of purpose.

Discovering that I could deliver messages from loved ones on the other side was like uncovering a hidden part of myself—a part that had always been there but only revealed itself when I needed it most. The first time it happened, I was overwhelmed by a sense of clarity and purpose I'd never felt before. In that moment, everything in my life made sense.

I could feel the weight of others' pain, the longing to reconnect with those who had passed, and I knew I had the ability to bridge that gap.

This gift holds deep meaning for me, because I know what it's like to be broken by loss. When my dad died, it felt as though the world had shattered around me. The grief was suffocating—a constant ache I couldn't escape. I remember feeling utterly lost, desperate for a sign that he was still with me. The silence that followed his death was deafening, and I would have given anything to hear his voice one more time, to feel his presence even briefly.

In those darkest moments, I often wished someone could reach out to him, someone who could tell me he was okay, that he was still watching over me. That's why, when I discovered I could connect with the other side, it felt like a calling. I didn't want anyone else to feel the same hollowness and despair I had experienced. If I could offer even a sliver of comfort to someone in pain—if I could be the person who delivers those messages of love and reassurance then perhaps I could help heal the wounds that loss leaves behind.

Each time I relay a message from a loved one, I think of my dad and how much it would have meant to me to hear from him in those early days after his passing. It's not just about the words I share, but about the hope and healing they carry. I've learned that grief can be an isolating experience, but it doesn't have to be. By helping others connect with their loved ones, I'm able to honour my dad's memory in a way that brings light into the lives of those struggling through their own darkness.

This gift has become my way of transforming personal pain into something meaningful—a way of ensuring that no one has to navigate the experience of loss alone. It's a responsibility I do not take lightly, and with every message I deliver, I do so with the awareness that it represents a step toward healing—for both myself and those I am supporting.

Today, I stand as a psychic medium, a bridge between this world and the next. What began as a simple visit to a medium with my wife revealed an extraordinary truth about myself, one that has reshaped my life in ways I never could have imagined. The energy that once surged chaotically through me has become a guiding force, a link between the seen and the unseen. Each day, I continue to learn, to grow, and to honour the gift I have been given.

* * *

'As a psychic medium, I have had the profound honour of connecting with countless individuals who have sought guidance and solace after losing their loved ones. The question I am asked the most is 'Are they ok'? The stories I share are not merely anecdotes, but genuine accounts of people who have come to see me in person, via Zoom, or over the phone—each carrying the heavy weight of grief. From parents mourning a child to partners coping with the absence of their beloved, every encounter has been a journey of healing. While there are too many stories to tell them all, each person has left our sessions with a renewed sense of hope and a clearer path ahead. These moments of connection and reassurance have helped them see that, despite their devastating losses, there is still light and love to be found in their lives.'

* * *

‘I would also like to share that when I connect with a loved one through psychic mediumship, I don’t just receive their messages—I often feel what they felt. Sometimes it’s a sharp ache in the chest, the strain of laboured breathing, or the dull pressure of a lingering illness from their final days. It’s not imagined; it’s a visceral echo of their passing that moves through me. This kind of connection is deeply meaningful, but also physically and emotionally exhausting. Holding space for that level of pain—even briefly—takes its toll. It reminds me that mediumship isn’t just about light and comfort; sometimes, it’s about bearing witness to and honouring suffering, so that healing can begin on both sides.’

* * *

‘It is important to recognise that the path through grief is deeply personal, and what brings comfort to one person may not resonate with another. While spiritual healing and psychic readings have brought solace and a sense of connection to many who have sought my guidance, these approaches are not the only means of healing, nor are they suitable for everyone. Each individual’s journey through loss is unique, and whether it’s through therapy, support groups, creative expression, or spending time with loved ones, finding what helps you is what truly matters. Ultimately, anything that brings even a glimmer of peace and helps you navigate the difficult terrain of grief can be a powerful force in the healing process and knowing 'They Are Ok'.

## Finding Help:

If you or someone you know is struggling with grief, here are some resources that may help. Here are some grief helplines and support services available in the UK:

1. **Cruse Bereavement Care**
   - **Helpline**: 0808 808 1677
   - **Website**: www.cruse.org.uk
   - Provides free and confidential support for anyone who is grieving.
2. **Samaritans**
   - **Helpline**: 116 123
   - **Website**: www.samaritans.org
   - Offers 24/7 emotional support for anyone in distress, including those experiencing grief.
3. **Child Bereavement UK**
   - **Helpline**: 0800 02 888 40
   - **Website**: www.childbereavementuk.org
   - Supports families and professionals when a child dies or when a child is grieving.
4. **Winston's Wish**
   - **Helpline**: 08088 020 021

- **Website**: www.winstonswish.org
- Provides support for bereaved children and their families.

5. **The Compassionate Friends**
    - **Helpline**: 0345 123 2304
    - **Website**: www.tcf.org.uk
    - Offers support to parents and families after the death of a child.
6. **Support Line**
    - **Helpline**: 01708 765200 (hours vary)
    - **Website**: www.supportline.org.uk
    - Provides confidential emotional support to children, young adults, and adults, including those dealing with grief.
7. **John Hughes Psychic Medium**
    - **Website:** John Hughes Psychic | Psychic Readings for Insight and Guidance
    - Provides personal 1-1 readings. Connect with your loved ones that have passed and find the answers that you seek.

These helplines provide essential support for those coping with the loss of a loved one, offering a compassionate ear and practical advice.

Remember, it's okay to seek help and to lean on others as you navigate the journey of grief. You are not alone.

www.ingramcontent.com/pod-product-compliance
Ingram Content Group UK Ltd.
Pitfield, Milton Keynes, MK11 3LW, UK
UKHW050308021225
465603UK00002B/5

9 798896 042846